Celebrate
WITH
BREAD BAKING

Preparing Cheese-Herb Babka, page 31

Celebrate

WITH

BREAD BAKING

ESSENTIAL RECIPES
FOR SPECIAL OCCASIONS

Jenny Prior

PHOTOGRAPHY BY LAURA FLIPPEN

ROCKRIDGE
PRESS

Interior and Cover Designer: Lisa Schreiber
Art Producer: Sue Bischofberger
Editor: Brian Sweeting
Production Editor: Rachel Taenzler
Photography © 2020 Laura Flippen. Author photo courtesy of Tori Wible.

ISBN: Print 978-1-64611-636-2 | eBook 978-1-64611-637-9
R0

To the bread makers
and the bread
breakers, this book
is for you. May the
recipes in this book
help you celebrate
with the people you
love in memorable
and delicious ways!

CLOCKWISE FROM LEFT: **Berry Scones,** page 41;
Skillet Cinnamon-Apple Bread, page 95;
Cheese-Herb Babka, page 31

CONTENTS

Preparing Mushroom Baozi, page 128

INTRODUCTION

Breaking bread together is something sacred. It creates joy, fosters community, and is the centerpiece of many family gatherings.

What memory springs to mind when you think of sharing bread? Our most meaningful experiences with bread often have to do with the heart and generosity of the baker, not necessarily their technical abilities.

At least that's my story. Both my grandmas grew up poor, one during the Great Depression. Despite the simplicity of their cooking, they created a powerful legacy of love and family in their kitchens.

Whenever we would visit my dad's parents as young kids, my grandma made the most delicious blueberry muffins with a sweet crumbly topping that she would serve in a beautiful silver breadbasket lined with a cloth. It didn't matter that they were made from a box; they will always remind me of sitting in grandma and grandpa's sunny dining room and savoring a sweet moment together.

As I grew up, I discovered a love for baking and cooking. In my teen years, I made quick breads, muffins, and the like, but I discovered a love for sourdough bread baking after I became a mom. As I started to bake more and more bread, I would bring it to meetings, family get-togethers, and neighbors. It would spark conversations and foster delight.

At one memorial lunch gathering at my grandparents' house, there was a thick air of sadness, family politics, and anxiety. I was baking bread in the kitchen, the same kitchen where those blueberry muffins brought a sense of joy and belonging to my childhood. The atmosphere completely shifted as guests took fresh slices of bread with delighted anticipation.

My hope for you as you read this book is that you find inspiration and practical help to create breads for your family traditions and celebrations. This book includes a diverse collection of recipes for many holidays and across different cultures so that as many people as possible can find a recipe that brings them a sense of belonging and home. Each chapter is organized from easiest to most difficult recipes.

As you read this book, I hope that you find recipes to celebrate your family, friends, community, favorite holidays, and milestones, as well as a way to offer comfort to others in pain. It might surprise you how the bread you make will have an impact on the hearts of the people you share it with.

Chapter One

BREAD BASICS

To help you get started with bread making and review key concepts, this chapter includes a summary of key terms, leavening agents, bread-making techniques, and other helpful information.

Terminology and Process

The first important part of baking bread is learning how to talk and think like a baker. In this book, there are many different types of bread recipes with varying levels of difficulty. Some use yeast and include long periods of fermentation and proofing, whereas others are quick breads baked right after mixing. The following terms will give you a better understanding of the important steps and processes involved as you start baking.

Active/activate: This term refers to either proofing dried commercial yeast in warm liquid or feeding a sourdough starter and allowing it to become active over the course of several hours.

Autolyse: The step of mixing flour and water together to allow the flour to become fully hydrated so that gluten can develop strength and structure without a long kneading period.

Baking powder: A combination of baking soda, an acidic element, and a stabilizer. Once mixed with liquid in a recipe, it causes a reaction that releases bubbles of carbon dioxide. It is used to leaven quick breads and cakes.

Baking soda: A base ingredient that is combined with acidic ingredients (e.g., lemon juice, buttermilk, yogurt, honey, chocolate) to create a reaction that releases carbon dioxide bubbles. It is used in cookies, as well as in quick breads and cakes where an acidic ingredient is present.

Crumb: The texture of the bread, as well as the look of the interior when a loaf is cut in half. The crumb can be described as even (texture and holes of even size and shape), uneven (some large gaping holes and some denser areas), loose or open (lots of holes), or tight (small holes, tighter together).

Feeding the starter (also known as "refreshing" or "discard and feed"): The cyclical process of adding fresh flour and water to a small amount of sourdough starter to maintain the health of the starter and allow it to become active for bread baking.

Fermentation (also referred to as "bulk fermentation," "allow dough to rise," or "first rise"): The span of time just after mixing the dough, when the dough expands as the yeast converts the sugar or carbohydrates in the dough to gas, increasing the volume of the dough and developing gluten strength.

Folding (also known as "stretch and fold"): A process to develop the gluten and dough strength, used for high hydration or wetter dough that can't be kneaded easily (e.g., ciabatta, sourdough boule). It is done by taking sections of dough, pulling the section over the bulk of the dough, then repeating with all sides of the dough.

Gluten: The protein in wheat flour that allows a dough to become elastic during the bread-making process.

Hydration: The ratio of liquid (e.g., water, milk) to total flour. Some bakers use percentages in baking. For example, equal parts liquid and flour, 1:1, results in 100 percent hydration. Most breads range from 50 percent to 75 percent hydration.

Leavening agent: A general term for the ingredient that makes dough rise (e.g., yeast, baking powder, baking soda).

Kneading: A process used to develop gluten and dough strength. It is done by successively folding the dough onto itself, pushing downward, and stretching the dough until the dough becomes cohesive and smooth and pulls away from the work surface.

Proofing (also referred to as "proving," "second rise," or "final rise"): The time given for a shaped bread to rise and expand in preparation for baking. This term is also used interchangeably with "activating" when prepping active dry yeast for baking.

Rest (also known as "bench rest"): The time given to allow the gluten in the dough to relax and regain elasticity before shaping.

Quick bread: A bread made with baking powder or baking soda that is baked soon after mixing without a fermentation or proofing period.

Scale: As a noun, this refers to the tool for measuring the weight of ingredients. As a verb, this refers to the act of weighing ingredients for a recipe. See also "tare."

Scoring: A cut or series of cuts made in the top of a loaf with a lame or bread knife before placing the dough in a hot oven. Scoring helps the bread expand, but it can also be used for decorative purposes.

Shaping: A process in bread making in which specific steps are followed to manipulate the dough into a shape (e.g., braid, round boule, baguette).

Tare: When using a scale, tare is used to deduct the bowl (or previously added ingredients) from the weight being measured on the scale. It is used each time a new ingredient is added.

Yeast: A single-celled microorganism that feeds on sugar and produces alcohol and carbon dioxide as byproducts to create leavened or rising breads.

Yeast bread: A bread that is made with yeast (i.e., active dry, quick/instant yeast, or sourdough starter) and requires periods of fermentation, shaping, and proofing.

What Are the Quick Bread Leaveners?

In quick breads, two types of leavening agents can be used: baking powder or baking soda. Baking soda is a base and requires an acidic element (e.g., buttermilk, lemon, honey) to create a reaction that produces carbon dioxide to make the quick bread rise.

Baking powder is comprised of a base (baking soda), an acidic element (cream of tartar), and a stabilizer (cornstarch). Because it has a base and an acidic element, it begins reacting when added to a liquid during the quick bread–mixing process. Baking powder has a neutral flavor and can be found in single-acting or double-acting varieties. Single-acting baking powder begins reacting once mixed and should be baked right away. Double-acting has two stages of reactivity: first when mixed with liquid and second when baked in a hot oven.

Measuring and Scaling

Flour can settle differently based on how long it has sat, how much air is in it, or how it was scooped for measurement. The ratio of wet ingredients to dry ingredients is very important in bread recipes, and too much variation in your measurements can lead to problems with texture, flavor, and shape.

To avoid the variability of measuring by volume, use a kitchen scale to give you the best accuracy in your bread baking. It may seem unfamiliar to many American bakers, but after you begin measuring this way, you may begin to prefer it!

When using a digital food scale, place the container on the scale and tare the weight. This will bring the total to 0 grams. Each time you add one ingredient and see the scale register the correct amount, tare your scale again to bring it back to zero for the next ingredient. Measure the liquids first because it's easier to remove excess liquid if you accidentally add too much; once flour is added, it's nearly impossible to take out any extra liquid.

Temperatures and Calculations

The activity of yeast or other leavening agents is heavily influenced by temperature.

Yeast thrives in warm environments. When adding water, it should be between 105°F and 110°F for active dry yeast, between 70°F and 100°F for instant yeast, or between 60°F and 90°F for a starter or preferment. The warm water will create optimal conditions for yeast development

WORKING WITH DIFFERENT FLOURS

All-purpose flour and bread flour are most commonly used for bread baking because of their versatility and their high percentage of gluten protein, which results in a stronger dough and better rise.

Another white flour is cake flour, which is helpful in some quick breads like scones and biscuits. It has a low percentage of gluten protein, making it great for creating a flaky or crumbly texture.

Whole-wheat flours have many different varieties. Whole wheat creates a more flavorful bread with more fiber and a chewier texture, depending on how much is added to a recipe. It requires a higher level of hydration because flour containing the bran of the wheat absorbs more liquid.

in the dough, but water temperatures above 130°F will kill the yeast.

The air temperature and humidity in the room affect the dough development, as well. A warm room will speed up the fermentation process, which can require monitoring or adjustments (e.g., using the refrigerator to slow the fermentation and develop more flavor). A cold room will make the fermentation time longer—this is important to remember in winter months.

In some situations, a cold environment created by a refrigerator can be useful. The slower fermentation creates complex flavors, allows flexibility for the baker if they need to delay the next step, and can allow a shaped bread to proof slower so it can be baked first thing in the morning.

Some bakers like to use the following formula to calculate the best water temperature to use to ensure Desired Dough Temperature (DDT), which is a range of 74°F to 78°F. This formula multiplies the middle of the DDT range (76°F) by the number of variables in the recipe (air temperature, water temperature, friction factor, and sometimes the preferment/starter temperature). It then deducts the known variables to find the needed water temperature.

[DDT 76°F x 3] – [air temperature + flour temperature + friction factor] = water temperature

When using a preferment or sourdough starter, there is a fourth variable to consider, so the calculation changes to the following:

[DDT 76°F x 4] – [air temperature + preferment temperature + flour temperature + friction factor] = water temperature

The friction factor depends on the mixing method. For hand mixing it is 6°F to 8°F, and for machine mixing it is 15°F to 30°F (approximately 3°F per minute of machine mixing).

Kneading and Folding

To develop the gluten in yeast breads, kneading or folding techniques are used to strengthen the dough and accelerate the fermentation process.

Kneading is commonly used in bread recipes. It can be done by machine or by hand. When using a machine mixer, the time of kneading should be reduced to one-third or half the amount of time instructed for kneading by hand.

Folding accomplishes the same objective as kneading (a well-developed and strong dough), but it is typically used for high-hydration doughs that are wet or sticky, making them difficult to knead. Folding can be referred to as "stretch and fold," as well.

Rising and Fermentation

In yeast breads, the fermentation time, or rising time, is critical for making the best bread. This time allows the yeast to convert starches into sugars and to use those sugars to produce carbon dioxide gas. This process creates air in the dough, making it rise. It also allows the enzymes in the flour to continue making strong connections between gluten proteins.

Typically, there are two fermentation or rising periods. The first one is called bulk fermentation or first rise and takes place right after the dough is mixed and kneaded or folded. The second fermentation is called proofing or second rise and takes place after the dough has been shaped.

Shaping

After a yeast bread ferments, it is shaped according to the recipe. Shaping usually involves the following steps: dividing (for certain recipes), pre-shaping, resting, and final shaping.

A pre-shape is a gentle way of getting the dough in the approximate desired shape. The rest period that follows allows the gluten to relax, which makes the dough more flexible for final shaping.

Using a dough scraper is invaluable for dividing dough when necessary, releasing the dough from the work surface, and moving the dough. A dusting of flour can be useful when shaping certain kinds of dough to keep it from sticking.

Shaping requires manipulating the dough to produce structure and tension. The shaping creates structure for how the bread will proof and rise. The tension helps create strength on the outside of the dough, which is important for the final form.

WORKING WITH YEAST

There are two broad categories of yeast: commercial yeast and wild or naturally derived yeast (which is the yeast found in sourdough).

Commercial yeast can be purchased as active dry yeast or instant yeast. These are dormant until activated by water. Commercial yeast should be stored in the refrigerator or freezer to extend its shelf life. Open packages of yeast should be used within 4 months if kept in the refrigerator or within 6 months if kept in the freezer.

The wild yeast found in sourdough is living and active, not dormant like commercial yeast, so it requires regular maintenance. Home bakers can keep an active sourdough starter stored in the refrigerator and refresh it at least once per week to keep it alive and healthy.

Proofing

Proofing (also known as the second rise) is the final step before baking your bread. This step allows the bread to grow in volume in its shaped form.

Proofing is ideally done in a warm place. It can be done in a cold environment like a refrigerator for flavor development, but the time needed will be four to five times longer than proofing at room temperature. When done correctly, the crumb of the bread will be even and soft. Underproofed bread results in a tight, dense crumb. Overproofed bread usually has gaping holes, has an uneven crumb, and barely rises during baking.

To test proofing, press a finger lightly onto the dough. (Dip your finger in water if the dough is sticky.) If the indentation remains but slowly rises back, it is ready. If the dough springs back quickly, it needs more time. If there is no spring back and the indentation remains unchanged or starts to cave in, the dough is overproofed.

Baking

Because modern home ovens are made to remove extra moisture and humidity from the oven, it is necessary to take care in creating a steamy oven, which is ideal for bread baking. Bread baked without steam won't rise well and will come out dense and with a thick, hard crust.

Steam in baking allows the bread dough to expand by keeping the crust soft in the first part of the bake. To create steam, place a metal pan filled with water on the lowest oven rack while the oven preheats. You can even add rolled-up towels soaked in water or lava rocks to the pan to create more steam. By the time the oven is preheated, the water should be steaming. Once the dough is placed in the oven, use a water spray bottle to give the

TIMING

Timing is important for yeast breads during their various fermentation periods. When using a preferment or starter, this time can range from 6 to 16 hours, depending on the method. The bulk fermentation, or first rise, takes 1 to 3 hours when using commercial yeast or 3 to 5 hours when using a starter. Proofing, or the second rise, requires usually half the amount of time as the bulk fermentation.

When planning your baking, it's important to account for mixing, kneading, baking, and cooling times, as well. Developing a sense of rhythm is key to becoming a successful baker. One tip is to write down the time each step of a recipe will take place before you begin so that you can plan your day without guessing or forgetting when to do the next step.

walls of the oven a quick spray to add an extra burst of steam. After the steamy portion of baking is done, the pan of water is removed and the bread continues to bake to create a golden, well-baked crust.

Lean breads (breads with little to no added oils or fat) are cooked at a high temperature, usually 450°F or higher. Enriched breads with added sugars and fat require baking at a lower temperature (350°F to 375°F) because the sugar makes them more susceptible to burning. Bread is perfectly baked when it presents these attributes: noticeable change in color (usually golden or dark brown), hollow sound when tapped on the bottom of the bread, and an internal bread temperature of 190°F to 200°F.

Cooling

After bread is removed from the oven, the baking process continues inside the bread. It must be given time to cool before cutting or serving. If cut too soon, the crumb will be sticky and the steam that escapes will impact the final texture of the bread.

Place bread on a cooling rack that allows air to circulate so that moisture from steam doesn't become trapped on the bottom. Most breads need an hour to cool before they should be cut.

STORING AND REVIVING

If the bread will be enjoyed within 1 to 3 days of baking, store at room temperature in a sealed container or plastic bag. To revive bread stored at room temperature, you can toast the bread, which brings back a fresh flavor, wrap the bread in a damp paper towel and microwave for 10 seconds, or warm it in the oven at 300°F to 325°F for 5 to 10 minutes with a few sprays from a water spray bottle on the oven walls at the start.

It is not recommended to store bread in the refrigerator, as the refrigerator dehumidifies, or pulls moisture out of, foods. However, breads can be frozen to save for a later time. To store bread in the freezer, it should be wrapped twice with freezer-grade foil and/or a plastic zip-top bag to prevent freezer burn. To revive frozen bread, place it in a warm oven (325°F to 350°F) for 20 to 60 minutes (the size of the bread will impact the duration) with a few sprays from a water spray bottle on the oven walls, until it is no longer frozen in the center.

Working with Starters

Starters are often used to add a more complex flavor or when making a naturally fermented bread like sourdough.

A starter is made by mixing flour and water with either a bit of existing sourdough starter or a small amount of commercial yeast. The mixture is then covered and left at room temperature for 6 to 16 hours, depending on the method. Over time, it becomes active, at least doubling in volume and producing lots of bubbles and a fragrant aroma.

In addition to creating a more complex flavor in bread, a starter will help bread last longer than breads made with a direct or straight dough method, which involves adding yeast directly into the dough at the time of mixing.

An important final note is that starter is often the general term for a sourdough starter, which is regularly refreshed to maintain the health and activity of the microorganisms (natural/wild yeast and lactic acid bacteria). Using a sourdough starter in bread making is my preferred method. When I've done side-by-side comparisons using a direct dough–method bread, a bread made with a starter with commercial yeast, and a bread made with a sourdough starter, the flavor of the sourdough starter–based bread has won every time. Most of the

TROUBLESHOOTING: BAKING AT DIFFERENT ALTITUDES

At high altitudes (3,500 feet or higher), the lower air pressure can cause bread and other baked items to over-expand, collapse during baking, or come out with a dry or gummy texture. To prevent this, here are some recommended adjustments you can follow.

During the bulk fermentation, the dough should only be left to expand until it doubles, which might take less time than the recipe instructs.

For quick bread recipes, reduce the amount of baking powder or baking soda by one-eighth to one-quarter per whole teaspoon. Try the following adjustments: Reduce the amount of sugar by 1 to 4 tablespoons per cup of sugar, reduce the amount of butter or oil by 1 to 3 tablespoons, increase the amount of water or milk by 1 to 4 tablespoons per cup of liquid, and occasionally increase the amount of flour by 2 to 4 tablespoons. Start with reducing by the smallest amount; generally the high end of the adjustments given is for altitudes of 5,000 feet and higher.

For yeast bread recipes, you may have to increase the amount of liquid added to create the correct texture. Increase the baking temperature by 15°F for enriched breads and 25°F for lean breads with little to no fat, and decrease the baking time by 5 to 10 minutes.

recipes in this book are starter-based; however I include instructions for working with commercial yeast in the recipes, as well as directions for adding commercial yeast after the sourdough-based starter/levain is added, to shorten the fermentation times. If you'd like your bread solely made with sourdough, see the recipe tips for the sourdough-only timings.

Skills and Techniques

Some essential skills and techniques for bread making include time planning, note-taking, folding, kneading, and shaping.

Note-taking is a skill that complements time planning. Use a notebook to take notes about your bakes, the time needed for different steps, temperatures

TIME PLANNING TEMPLATE

Because this book is written with holidays and special occasions in mind, most of the recipes require special planning. As you envision your event, start with the time you want your bread ready to enjoy, then work backward:

- **Bread ready by:** . . . . _____
- **Bread ready by time – cooling time = bread out of oven by:** . . . . _____
- **Bread out of oven time – baking duration = bread finished proofing and into oven:** . . . . _____
- **Bread finished proofing and into oven time – proofing duration = start of proof:** . . . . _____
- **Start of proof time – average of 40 minutes of shaping = end of bulk ferment:** . . . . _____
- **End of bulk ferment time – duration of bulk ferment = start of bulk ferment:** . . . . _____
- **Start of bulk ferment time – average of 20 minutes for mixing and kneading = start of mixing:** . . . . _____
- **Start of mixing time – activation time for starter (when applicable) = starter preparation time:** . . . . _____

The times for fermentation, shaping, and proofing can be taken out if you'd like to use these guidelines for quick breads.

of water or the room in which you're baking, variations you tried, and other details that seem useful.

Kneading and folding (see the section Kneading and Folding on page 5) are important for dough development and strength. To knead dough by hand, push, roll, stretch, and apply pressure to the dough against a strong work surface. The dough will become cohesive and smooth and will release from the work surface easily when it has been sufficiently kneaded.

Shaping (see the section Shaping on page 6) is a skill that takes repeated practice to improve. However, here are some general recommendations.

When dough is wet or sticky, move the dough with small, quick movements using your hand and/or dough scraper; otherwise the dough will stick. If your recipe calls for an unfloured surface, place a bowl of water nearby so that you can occasionally dip your hand or scraper. Similarly, if your recipe calls for a floured surface, place a small bowl of flour nearby for reapplying.

Equipment

Baking bread becomes much easier when you have the right tools. The following are some recommendations for supplies to purchase that are listed in two categories: must-haves and nice-to-haves.

MUST-HAVES

Must-have items are helpful for general bread baking and will be used in nearly every bread recipe.

Bowl covers: To cover your bowl of dough, use a clean, moistened kitchen towel, beeswax wrap, an unused shower cap, or plastic wrap.

Digital food scale: Bread making becomes much easier and more accurate with the use of a food scale.

Large cast-iron skillet: A 10- or 12-inch cast-iron skillet is important for many of the flat breads, as well as some of the shaped breads.

Large mixing bowls: One large mixing bowl will help you get started with mixing your breads. Ceramic, glass, or stainless steel are all great options.

Loaf pan: A loaf pan is used for many of the quick breads in this book. Metal or aluminum is common. Cast-iron, glass, or silicone loaf pans also work well.

Metal pan for steam: Steam is an integral part of bread baking, so a metal pan, such as a brownie or roasting pan with a depth of 2 to 3 inches, is ideal for filling with water and creating steam in the oven. Using an unbreakable pan is important.

Oven mitts: High heat–resistant oven mitts will keep your hands and arms safe when moving bread in and out of the hot oven. My favorite are lined, silicone oven mitts because they can get wet on the outside and still provide protection.

Parchment paper: Parchment paper is excellent for baking and cooking. It allows items to bake without sticking to the pan and can also be used to wrap some breads, line a gift basket, or line loaf pans.

Plastic dough scraper: A plastic dough scraper is an essential tool that is versatile, helpful, and inexpensive. Having a dough scraper with one straight side and one rounded side is ideal.

Rolling pin: A rolling pin is used in several recipes to roll out dough. This item is a must-have because it is difficult to find a good substitute.

Serrated bread knife: If a sharp serrated bread knife isn't already in your kitchen, this investment is important for convenience and, more importantly, for safety. Look for a scalloped edge, which is made to cut cleanly through bread, rather than a jagged edge, which can catch on the bread and cause injury.

Water spray bottle: Buy a generic spray bottle and fill it with water. Use it to spray the sides of the oven before baking, to create steam.

NICE-TO-HAVES

These nice-to-have items are recommended to save time and energy. This list also includes items that are needed for specialized recipes.

Aluminum foil: This is helpful for certain recipes and for loosely covering bread if the top is browning too quickly.

Baking stone: A baking stone helps create even and sustained heat for shaped loaves. You can bake directly on a baking sheet instead, but timing might change slightly.

Bamboo steamer with liners: A bamboo steamer with parchment liners is needed for making steamed rolls.

Bread lame: This tool is helpful when scoring loaves of bread.

Corrugated panettone molds: To make panettone or kulich, specialized molds will give you the best results.

Disposable loaf pans: One-time-use loaf pans, available in standard and small sizes, are excellent for gifting quick bread loaves.

Dutch oven: A cast-iron Dutch oven that has at least a 4-quart capacity is a bread baker's secret for creating a beautiful hot, steamy environment for round breads at home. Cast iron radiates even heat, and the heavy lid helps trap steam inside the pot during baking.

Electric dough mixer: This is a large purchase and not essential, but it makes mixing and kneading much easier and faster.

Large plastic container: A large plastic container with a minimum 4-quart capacity is nice to have when doing a bulk ferment if you'd like to measure the rise of the dough or place the dough in the refrigerator to slow the ferment.

Large pot: A large metal or enamel-covered cast-iron pot with at least a 4-quart capacity can be used for warming milk for certain recipes, heating oil for frying, and boiling water for poaching bagels or pretzels.

Lefse-making kit: Lefse is a bread unique to Norway and is a special family tradition for the winter season, especially at Christmas. To make this bread, this specialized kit is recommended and includes a cloth for rolling the dough, a cloth-covered rolling pin, sticks for transferring the rolled lefse, and a special pan. See the recipe on page 130 for tips on making lefse without a kit.

Round proofing basket/bowl: Usually made with coiled rattan or another breathable material, this tool will help you proof round loaves for baking. An alternative is to use a colander lined with a kitchen towel.

Sourdough starter: Many recipes in this book use sourdough starter, which can be made at home in 7 days or bought online.

Waffle maker: If you plan to make waffles, you will need this tool.

Pane di Pasqua, page 29

Chapter Two

SPRING

Spring is a season of renewal, color, and celebration. The recipes in this section will give you ideas for fun ways to celebrate holidays with friends and family, including soda bread for St. Patrick's Day, bolani for Eid al-Fitr, beignets for Mardi Gras, malpua for Holi, and many more.

IRISH-INSPIRED SODA BREAD

Yield: 1 large loaf

PREP TIME: 15 MINUTES | **INACTIVE TIME:** 30 MINUTES | **BAKE TIME:** 30 TO 35 MINUTES

TOOLS NEEDED: food scale, large mixing bowl, spoon, liquid measuring cup or carafe, parchment paper, cast-iron skillet or flat baking sheet, knife, pastry brush

Traditional Irish-inspired soda bread comes together with little time and simple ingredients. It is often enjoyed on St. Patrick's Day and is incredible next to an Irish stew or corned beef and cabbage.

450 grams all-purpose flour (3 cups plus 3½ tablespoons)

125 grams whole-wheat flour (¾ cup plus 3 tablespoons)

9 grams baking soda (1½ teaspoons)

9 grams salt (1½ teaspoons)

30 grams white cane sugar, plus more for sprinkling (2 tablespoons) (optional)

430 grams buttermilk, plus extra to brush on bread (1¾ cups plus ½ table-spoon) (or substitute whole milk and freshly squeezed lemon juice, see step 3)

1. **PREHEAT:** Preheat the oven to 425°F.

2. **COMBINE THE DRY INGREDIENTS:** Combine the all-purpose flour, whole-wheat flour, baking soda, salt, and sugar (if using) in a large mixing bowl. Stir together with a spoon.

3. **ADD THE BUTTERMILK:** Pour the buttermilk into the dry mixture. If you don't have buttermilk, substitute whole milk and freshly squeezed lemon juice. Squeeze 2 tablespoons of lemon juice into a liquid measuring glass, then add whole milk until it equals 450 grams or just under 2 cups. Stir the mixture and let it sit for 5 minutes.

4. **MIX:** Stir the buttermilk into the dry ingredients until there are no dry patches left.

5. **PREPARE BAKING DISH:** Cut a large piece of parchment and lay it inside a large cast-iron skillet or on a flat baking sheet.

6. **SHAPE:** Turn the dough out onto a lightly floured surface. Using your hands, form the dough into a round shape. Place it in the center of the parchment and pat it down until the shaped dough is about 10 inches across. Cut a deep X-mark across the top of the loaf, about ½ inch deep in the center.

7. **BRUSH TOP:** Use a pastry brush to brush the extra buttermilk on the top, in the cut X, and all around the sides of the bread. Then sprinkle some additional sugar all over the crust (if using).

8. **BAKE:** Bake for 30 to 35 minutes. The bread should have a golden-brown top and a toothpick or knife inserted into the center should come out clean.

9. **COOL:** Allow the bread to cool for about 30 minutes before cutting into wedges.

PARAGUAYAN-INSPIRED CHIPA
(CHEESE BREAD)

Yield: 16 chipa rings or 32 chipa rolls

PREP TIME: 15 TO 25 MINUTES | **INACTIVE TIME:** 40 MINUTES | **BAKE TIME:** 14 TO 18 MINUTES

TOOLS NEEDED: large mixing bowl, spoon, food scale, cheese grater, parchment paper, 2 baking sheets, knife

This form of chipa *from Paraguay is also known as* chipa argolla. *It is very popular as part of Easter or Holy Week and is traditionally given to neighbors as a sign of generosity and celebration. This bread is a delicious option to make for friends or neighbors who cannot eat gluten.*

4 large eggs

160 grams mozzarella cheese, grated (1¾ cups, loosely filled)

64 grams Parmesan cheese, freshly grated (¾ cup, loosely filled)

2 grams anise seeds (1 teaspoon) (optional)

6 grams salt (1 teaspoon)

248 grams milk (1 cup plus 1 tablespoon)

72 grams oil, such as avocado oil or olive oil (⅓ cup)

360 grams cassava flour (2 cups)

96 grams cornmeal (½ cup)

2 grams baking powder (½ teaspoon)

Sea salt flakes, for topping (optional)

1. **BEAT THE EGGS:** Beat the eggs in a large mixing bowl with a spoon.
2. **ADD THE CHEESES:** Mix in the grated mozzarella, the Parmesan, and the anise seeds (if using). Add the salt, milk, and oil, mixing to combine.
3. **ADD THE DRY INGREDIENTS:** Add the cassava flour, cornmeal, and baking powder. Mix until a soft dough is formed.
4. **CHILL THE DOUGH:** Cover the bowl and allow the dough to chill in the refrigerator for 20 minutes.
5. **PREPARE THE BAKING SHEETS:** While the dough is chilling, place two large pieces of parchment on top of two flat baking sheets.
6. **PREHEAT:** Preheat the oven to 425°F.
7. **DIVIDE THE DOUGH:** Turn the dough out onto a work surface. Divide the dough into quarters, then divide each quarter of dough into four pieces, making 16 pieces total. Roll each piece into a ball. (See tips for how to make 32 rolls instead of rings.)
8. **SHAPE THE RINGS:** On your work surface, roll each piece into a 6-inch-long rope. Bring

CONTINUED ON NEXT PAGE

the ends of the rope together and seal to form a ring shape. If there are cracks in the ring or it comes apart, pinch the broken sections of dough back together with your fingers. Place the rings 2 inches apart on the parchment-lined baking sheets. If your dough becomes too warm or soft and won't hold its shape, chill for 5 to 10 minutes, covered.

9. **BAKE:** Sprinkle the chipa with flaked sea salt (if using). Bake the chipa for 14 to 18 minutes. The rings should look baked with golden-brown bubbles of cheese that have formed on the outside.

10. **COOL:** Allow the chipa to cool for 20 minutes, then serve warm.

TIPS: To make 32 rolls instead of 16 rings, divide your dough into 32 pieces and roll each piece into a ball. The baking time will be 10 to 14 minutes.
Chipa can be made ahead and frozen after shaping. Bake as directed in step 9 without thawing.

VEGETARIAN BOLANI

Yield: 8 Bolani

PREP TIME: 60 TO 85 MINUTES | **INACTIVE TIME:** 50 MINUTES | **BAKE TIME:** 3 TO 5 MINUTES PER BATCH

TOOLS NEEDED: medium or large pot, knife, colander, food scale, large bowl, spoon, cutting board, potato masher (substitute forks or electronic mixer, if needed), rolling pin, 10-inch skillet, serving plate, paper towels, metal or wood spatula, small bowl

Bolani have an incredible savory flavor and combination of textures— crispy on the outside with soft potatoes inside. Bolani are a filled bread from Afghanistan and are a great way to celebrate Eid al-Fitr, but they are delicious all year long as an appetizer or a vegetarian entrée.

FOR THE DOUGH
240 grams water (1 cup)
10 grams olive oil (1 tablespoon)
450 grams all-purpose flour (3 cups plus 3½ tablespoons)
50 grams whole-wheat flour (⅓ cup)
10 grams salt (1½ teaspoons)

FOR THE FILLING
2 medium russet potatoes, peeled and quartered (400 to 450 grams, after peeling)

2 tablespoons olive oil
1½ teaspoons salt
1 teaspoon freshly ground black pepper
½ cup chopped cilantro
½ cup chopped scallions

FOR FRYING
¼ cup olive or avocado oil

FOR THE YOGURT SAUCE
1 cup plain whole milk Greek yogurt

1 to 2 garlic cloves, minced
3 to 4 tablespoons minced fresh dill
½ teaspoon ground coriander
½ teaspoon salt
1 to 2 tablespoons water, as needed

1. **COOK THE POTATOES:** Bring a large pot of water to a boil. Add the potatoes, reduce to a simmer, and cover. Cook for 20 to 25 minutes, until the potatoes are fork-tender. Once the potatoes are cooked, immediately strain using a colander, then rinse under cool water to prevent overcooking.

2. **WEIGH THE DOUGH INGREDIENTS:** While the potatoes are boiling, weigh the water and oil for the dough in a mixing bowl. Add the all-purpose flour, whole-wheat flour, and salt. Mix until the liquids are absorbed.

3. **KNEAD THE DOUGH:** Turn the dough out onto a work surface and knead for 10 minutes. If the dough seems too dry after 2 to 3 minutes of kneading, add water 1 teaspoon at a time. Cover the dough and set aside for 20 to 30 minutes to rest.

CONTINUED ON NEXT PAGE

4. **MAKE THE FILLING:** Place the potatoes in a bowl. Add the olive oil, salt, and pepper and mash well until the potatoes are smooth with a few small lumps. Mix the cilantro and scallions into the mashed potatoes.

5. **DIVIDE:** Divide the dough into 8 equal pieces. Roll each piece into a ball and cover with a kitchen towel.

6. **SHAPE AND FILL:** Lightly flour your work surface. Take one ball of dough and roll until very thin, similar to a tortilla. Take one-eighth of the filling (3 to 4 tablespoons) and place on one half of the rolled dough, leaving a ½-inch border. Fold the other half of the dough over the filling and press the edges together to seal. Remove any air trapped inside by gently pressing down on the top as you seal. Repeat with the remaining dough.

7. **HEAT THE OIL:** In a large skillet (at least 10 inches wide) over medium-high heat, heat the oil for frying. The oil should be hot enough that the bolani sizzle and have small bubbles when they are added, but not so high that the oil starts smoking. Line a plate with a paper towel and set aside.

8. **FRY THE BOLANI:** Put 2 bolani into the hot oil, folded edge to folded edge. Fry for 1 to 3 minutes, until golden and crispy on the bottom side, then flip and cook for 1 to 2 more minutes. Use a metal or wooden spatula to move the cooked bolani to the set-aside plate to drain. Repeat with the rest of the bolani. Add oil to the skillet if necessary, and allow the oil to come back up to temperature before continuing to fry.

9. **MAKE YOGURT SAUCE:** Mix together the Greek yogurt, garlic, dill, coriander, and salt until well combined. If the sauce is too thick, add water 1 tablespoon at a time until it reaches your desired consistency.

10. **COOL AND SERVE:** Allow the bolani to cool for 30 minutes, then serve warm with the yogurt sauce.

TIPS: Parsley, dill, or another herb can be substituted for cilantro in the filling.
Other types of potatoes can be substituted for the russet potatoes used here. You could even use sweet potatoes.

MALPUA

Yield: 18 to 20 malpua

PREP TIME: 25 MINUTES | **INACTIVE TIME:** 20 MINUTES | **BAKE TIME:** 40 TO 75 MINUTES

TOOLS NEEDED: food scale, mixing bowl, spoon, small pot, 2 plates,
paper towels, small saucepan, metal spoon or spatula

---

*Malpua are a traditional dish for celebrating Holi. The crunchy, chewy
texture, aromatic spices, and sweet syrup are an incredible combination.
They are so festive and perfect for celebrating the festival of colors.*

FOR THE DOUGH
175 grams all-purpose
flour (1½ cups)

1 gram ground carda-
mom (½ teaspoon)

1 gram ground fennel
(1 teaspoon)

200 grams whole milk
(¾ cup plus 2 tablespoons)

50 grams water
(3½ tablespoons)

FOR THE SIMPLE SYRUP
½ cup white cane sugar

¼ cup water

¼ teaspoon
ground cardamom

FOR FRYING
5 to 6 tablespoons ghee, divided

FOR THE GARNISH
¼ cup dry roasted pista-
chios or almonds, sliced
or chopped (optional)

2 tablespoons edible dried
rose petals (optional)

1. **WEIGH AND MIX THE DRY INGREDIENTS:**
   Measure the flour, cardamom, and fennel
   into a mixing bowl. Mix well to combine.

2. **ADD THE WET INGREDIENTS:** Pour in the milk
   and water. Mix well until smooth and thin
   enough to be poured. If the mixture is not
   thin enough, add 10 more grams of water,
   then stir. Repeat as needed.

3. **LET THE BATTER REST:** Set the batter aside to
   rest for 15 to 20 minutes.

4. **MAKE THE SIMPLE SYRUP:** Put the sugar and
   water in a small pot. Warm over medium
   heat, stirring frequently, until the sugar is
   dissolved and the texture turns syrupy. Stir
   in the cardamom. Set aside.

5. **PREPARE PLATES:** Place two layers of paper
   towels on a plate for the freshly fried
   malpua to drain on. Place a second plate to
   the side for serving. Create an assembly line
   with batter first, then a small saucepan, the
   paper towel–lined plate, the pot of simple
   syrup, and the serving plate.

6. **HEAT THE PAN AND MELT THE GHEE:** Heat
   3 tablespoons of ghee in the saucepan over
   medium heat. Once the ghee has melted,
   the bottom of the pan should be covered up
   to ¼ inch or so. Add the remaining 2 to 3
   tablespoons of ghee as needed.

CONTINUED ON NEXT PAGE

7. **FRY THE MALPUA:** When the ghee is melted and hot (see tips), drop 1 tablespoon of batter into the center of the pan. Do not try to stir or spread the batter; the batter should be thin enough to spread on its own. You can make 3 or 4 at a time depending on the pan size. After 2 minutes, the edges should be golden brown. Flip the malpua with a metal spoon or spatula, then cook for another 2 minutes. Ideally, the malpua should puff up after being flipped. Place the fried malpua on the paper towel–lined plate to drain off any excess ghee. Repeat with the remaining batter.

8. **SOAK THE MALPUA IN SIMPLE SYRUP:** Put 1 to 3 malpuas at a time in to the pot of simple syrup, flip to coat, then let any excess syrup drip off before placing on the serving plate.

9. **GARNISH AND SERVE:** Top the malpua with pistachios and edible rose petals (if using) and serve warm.

TIPS: Temperature is critical when frying dough. If the ghee is too cool, the batter will absorb too much fat, making them heavy and chewy instead of light and crispy. Using an infrared or candy thermometer, make sure the ghee is heated adequately, to 380ºF to 400ºF, before adding batter. The ghee should maintain a temperature of 350ºF to 380ºF when the batter is added—the temperature will increase back to the higher level after a few moments.
To avoid overheating the ghee, stand by when heating the pan and be ready to cook the malpua right after the pan reaches the correct temperature. Add batter at a regular rhythm, not letting the pan sit empty too long to avoid any overheating issues.

SOFT HERB POTATO ROLLS

Yield: 12 large rolls

PREP TIME: 45 TO 65 MINUTES | **INACTIVE TIME:** 13 TO 20 HOURS | **BAKE TIME:** 30 TO 40 MINUTES

TOOLS NEEDED: food scale, bowl, small pot, potato peeler, knife, large pot, colander, large bowl, potato masher, spoon, saucepan, candy thermometer or digital thermometer, parchment paper, baking sheet, plastic dough scraper, pastry brush

Warm, soft, and fragrant, these rolls will be a bright yet comforting part of any celebration! These soft herb potato rolls can be enjoyed alongside an Easter brunch or a family dinner or topped with sandwich ingredients for a picnic lunch.

FOR THE STARTER

15 grams sourdough starter (1 tablespoon) or ⅛ teaspoon instant yeast

110 grams water (¼ cup plus 3½ tablespoons)

110 grams all-purpose flour (¾ cup)

FOR THE DOUGH

80 grams mashed potatoes (from 2 medium to large potatoes; ¼ cup, after mashing)

80 grams milk (5 tablespoons)

110 grams warm water, divided (¼ cup plus 3½ tablespoons)

28 grams unsalted butter, at room temperature (2 tablespoons)

5 grams white cane sugar (1 teaspoon)

3 grams instant yeast (1 teaspoon) (may be omitted—see Focaccia Picnic Sandwiches tips on page 55)

200 grams starter (about 1 cup)

340 grams all-purpose flour (2¼ cups plus 3 tablespoons)

40 grams whole-wheat flour (¼ cup)

8 grams salt (1½ teaspoons)

8 grams fresh chives, minced (2 tablespoons)

4 grams fresh dill, minced (1 tablespoon)

FOR THE TOPPING

4 tablespoons unsalted butter, melted

1. **MAKE THE STARTER:** Around 8 to 12 hours before mixing your dough, combine the sourdough starter or yeast, water, and all-purpose flour in a bowl. Mix well, cover, and leave at room temperature to allow the yeast to activate. It will become bubbly and double in volume.

2. **COOK THE POTATOES:** Peel and quarter the potatoes. Bring a medium or large pot of water to a boil and add the potatoes. Reduce the heat to a simmer and cover the pot. Cook for 20 to 25 minutes, until the potatoes are fork-tender. Once the potatoes are finished cooking, immediately strain them using a colander and run them under cool water to stop any further cooking.

3. **MASH THE POTATOES:** Put 80 grams of potatoes in a mixing bowl and mash until there are almost no lumps. Don't over-mash them at this stage.

CONTINUED ON NEXT PAGE

4. **WARM THE MILK:** Heat the milk until it reaches a temperature of 115°F to 120°F.

5. **WEIGH THE INGREDIENTS:** Tare the bowl of mashed potatoes and add 70 grams of warm milk, 100 grams of warm water, and the butter. Add the sugar and instant yeast and allow the yeast to dissolve. Add 200 grams of the prepared starter, the all-purpose flour, and the whole-wheat flour.

6. **MIX:** Mix the ingredients together until a shaggy dough is formed, then add the salt, the remaining 10 grams of water, and the minced chives and dill. Mix to combine.

7. **KNEAD:** Knead the dough for 10 to 15 minutes by hand or for 3 to 8 minutes in a stand mixer with a dough hook on the lowest two speeds, until the dough is smooth, is no longer sticky, and releases easily from the bowl or work surface.

8. **BULK FERMENT:** Cover the dough and allow to ferment for 1½ to 2 hours, until doubled in volume.

9. **PREPARE THE BAKING SHEET:** Cut a large piece of parchment and place it on a flat baking sheet.

10. **DIVIDE:** Turn the dough out onto a lightly floured work surface and divide into 12 equal pieces.

11. **SHAPE:** Pat each piece of dough into a flat disc, then tuck the edges into the center, pinching to seal. Turn over onto the seam and roll under your hand briskly to tighten the roll into a ball. Place the rolls on the parchment paper–lined baking sheet at least 2 inches apart.

12. **PROOF:** Cover the rolls with a cloth or plastic wrap and allow to proof for 30 to 60 minutes, until the rolls are puffy and at least 1½ times larger.

13. **PREHEAT:** Preheat the oven to 375°F.

14. **BAKE:** Place the baking sheet in the preheated oven. Bake for 30 to 40 minutes, until the rolls are golden brown on top.

15. **ADD THE MELTED BUTTER:** Generously brush the melted butter all over the tops of the rolls.

16. **COOL:** Let the rolls cool for at least 20 minutes. Transfer to a plate to serve.

TIP: To speed up the potato prep, you can use the microwave instead of boiling potatoes. Prepare the potatoes as directed, then put them in a glass bowl with 1 tablespoon of water and cover with plastic wrap. Microwave on high for 8 to 10 minutes, until fork-tender. Leave in the microwave to cool for 5 to 10 minutes before continuing with the rest of the recipe.

MOROCCAN-INSPIRED ANISE-ORANGE BLOSSOM ROLLS

Yield: 16 rolls

PREP TIME: 60 TO 75 MINUTES | **INACTIVE TIME:** 3 TO 4 HOURS | **BAKE TIME:** 20 TO 25 MINUTES

TOOLS NEEDED: food scale, candy thermometer or digital thermometer, saucepan or small pot, large bowl, spoon, plastic dough scraper, parchment paper, 2 baking sheets, rolling pin, small bowl or cup, pastry brush, cooling rack

---

These sweet rolls are a great way to celebrate Eid al-Fitr. Orange blossom water is a special ingredient that can be found in Middle Eastern grocery stores or online. You can substitute rose water for a different flavor or omit it entirely for a plainer sweet roll.

FOR THE DOUGH

340 grams milk (1⅓ cups)

100 grams white cane sugar (½ cup)

12 grams instant yeast (1 tablespoon)

700 grams all-purpose flour (4⅔ cups)

6 grams salt (1 teaspoon)

2 large eggs

113 grams unsalted butter, melted (½ cup)

8 grams anise seeds (2 teaspoons)

14 to 28 grams orange blossom water (1 to 2 tablespoons)

FOR THE EGG WASH

1 large egg

⅛ teaspoon water

2 to 3 teaspoons golden sesame seeds, for topping

---

1. **WARM THE MILK:** Heat the milk until it reaches a temperature of 115°F to 120°F.

2. **WEIGH THE INGREDIENTS:** Pour 320 grams of the warm milk in a mixing bowl. Tare the scale, then add the sugar, instant yeast, and all-purpose flour.

3. **MIX:** Mix the ingredients together until a shaggy dough is formed, then add the salt and eggs. Stir, then add the slightly warm melted butter, anise seeds, and orange blossom water to taste. Mix to combine.

4. **KNEAD:** Turn the dough out onto your work surface and knead for 10 to 15 minutes by hand or for 4 to 8 minutes on low in a stand mixer, until the dough is smooth, is no longer sticky, and releases easily from the bowl or work surface.

5. **BULK FERMENT:** Cover the dough and allow to ferment for 2 to 2½ hours, until doubled in volume.

CONTINUED ON NEXT PAGE

6. **PREPARE THE BAKING SHEETS:** Place two large pieces of parchment paper on two flat baking sheets.

7. **DIVIDE:** Divide the dough into 16 equal pieces.

8. **SHAPE:** Roll one piece into a small disc with a rolling pin, then fold the edges in toward the center. Turn the dough over onto the seam and roll it into a smooth ball. Place the shaped ball of dough on the lined baking sheet. Repeat with the remaining pieces of dough, making sure to space the balls 2 to 3 inches apart on your baking sheet.

9. **PROOF:** Cover the rolls with plastic wrap and proof in a warm place for 1 to 1½ hours, until at least 1½ times larger.

10. **PREHEAT:** Preheat the oven to 400°F.

11. **PREPARE THE EGG WASH:** Mix together the egg and water in a small bowl or cup. Brush the egg wash onto the tops of the rolls with a pastry brush, then sprinkle golden sesame seeds on top.

12. **BAKE:** Bake for 20 to 25 minutes, until the rolls are a burnished brown color on the outside.

13. **COOL:** Cool the rolls on a cooling rack for at least 30 minutes before serving.

TIPS: Make sure your orange blossom water is fresh and fragrant. If it is old or spoiled, it will have a harsh mothball smell.
Ground anise seeds may be substituted for whole anise seeds.

BEIGNETS

Yield : 20 beignets

PREP TIME: 60 TO 75 MINUTES | **INACTIVE TIME:** 2 TO 3 HOURS
BAKE TIME: 2 TO 3 MINUTES PER BATCH

TOOLS NEEDED: food scale, saucepan or small pot, candy thermometer or digital thermometer, 2 large bowls, spoon, plastic dough scraper, rolling pin, pizza cutter or knife, medium pot, paper towels, cooling rack, timer, large slotted metal spoon (spatula may be substituted)

These beignets are delicious! Invite friends or neighbors over to enjoy these hot and fresh with a cup of coffee. Beignets are traditionally served for Mardi Gras but would make a special breakfast treat or dessert any time of year.

FOR THE DOUGH
180 grams milk (⅔ cup)

30 grams white cane sugar (2 tablespoons)

4 grams instant yeast (1 teaspoon)

350 grams all-purpose flour (2⅓ cups)

3 grams salt (½ teaspoon)

1 large egg

4 grams vanilla extract (1 teaspoon)

1 gram baking powder (¼ teaspoon)

56 grams unsalted butter, melted (¼ cup)

FOR FRYING
3 to 4 cups oil, such as vegetable oil, coconut oil, or tallow

FOR DUSTING
2 cups powdered sugar

1. **WARM THE MILK:** Heat the milk until it reaches a temperature of 115°F to 120°F.

2. **WEIGH THE INGREDIENTS:** Tare the mixing bowl. Combine 160 grams of the warm milk, the sugar, and the instant yeast. Tare and add the flour.

3. **MIX:** Mix the ingredients together until a shaggy dough is formed, then add the salt, egg, vanilla, and baking powder. Stir, then add the melted butter. Mix to combine.

4. **KNEAD:** Turn the dough out onto a work surface and knead for 10 to 15 minutes by hand or for 4 to 8 minutes on low in a stand mixer, until the dough is smooth, is no longer sticky, and releases easily from the bowl or work surface.

5. **BULK FERMENT:** Cover the dough and allow to ferment for 1½ to 2 hours, until doubled in volume.

6. **SHAPE:** Very lightly flour a work surface, then roll the dough with a rolling pin into an 8-by-10-inch rectangle that is about ½-inch thick. Use a wheeled pizza cutter or knife to cut the dough into 2-by-2-inch squares.

CONTINUED ON NEXT PAGE

7. **PROOF:** Cover the beignets with a cloth and proof for 15 to 30 minutes while you heat the oil for frying.

8. **HEAT THE OIL:** Attach a thermometer to the side of a medium pot that is at least 2.75-quart capacity. Pour in the oil until the depth is at least 3 inches and heat until the oil reaches 360°F.

9. **PREPARE A COOLING RACK:** While the oil is coming to temperature, line a cooling rack with paper towels and have a large slotted spoon and timer ready.

10. **PREPARE A BOWL FOR DUSTING:** Put the powdered sugar in a large bowl and set aside.

11. **FRY THE BEIGNETS:** Add 3 beignets at a time to the hot oil and cook for 1 to 1½ minutes, until the bottom side is browned. Use a metal slotted spoon to flip them and fry on the other side for another 1 to 1½ minutes. Transfer the beignets to the lined cooling rack to drain. Repeat until all the beignets have been fried.

12. **GARNISH AND SERVE:** Add the warm (slightly cooled) beignets 4 to 6 at a time to the large bowl of powdered sugar. Gently toss to coat, then serve.

TIPS: The oil temperature needs to be monitored. If it's too high, your beignets will have undercooked centers. If it's too low, you'll end up with oily beignets. When frying, adding the raw beignets to the oil will cause a dip in temperature that will slowly increase back to 360°F. This dough can be made in advance and chilled in the refrigerator for up to 24 hours before shaping and frying.

PANE DI PASQUA
(EASTER EGG BREAD)

Yield: 1 large shaped bread (serves 10 to 12)

PREP TIME: 60 TO 75 MINUTES | **INACTIVE TIME:** 11 TO 15 HOURS | **BAKE TIME:** 25 TO 30 MINUTES

TOOLS NEEDED: food scale, 2 large bowls, small pot, candy thermometer or digital thermometer, spoon, zester, plastic dough scraper, saucepan, baking sheet, parchment paper, bowls for dying eggs, cup, pastry brush, small bowl, spray bottle

Pane di Pasqua, often referred to as Easter egg bread, is a lot of fun for kids and adults enjoying an Easter celebration together. Not only is this bread festive and beautiful, but it also has a delicious flavor and soft texture.

FOR THE STARTER

30 grams sourdough starter (2 tablespoons) or ⅛ teaspoon instant yeast

15 grams white cane sugar (1 tablespoon)

50 grams water (3½ tablespoons)

100 grams all-purpose flour (⅔ cup)

FOR THE DOUGH

130 grams milk (½ cup)

65 grams warm water, divided (¼ cup plus ½ tablespoon)

3 grams instant yeast (1 teaspoon) (may be omitted—see Focaccia Picnic Sandwiches tips on page 55)

80 grams white cane sugar (¼ cup plus 2½ tablespoons)

150 grams starter (about ¾ cup)

600 grams bread flour (4 cups)

2 large eggs

115 grams unsalted butter, melted (½ cup)

5 grams salt (¾ teaspoon)

Zest of 1 lemon

FOR THE DECORATIVE EGGS

4 to 5 uncooked eggs, for decoration

1 quart water per egg color

1 tablespoon salt per egg color

2 tablespoons white vinegar per egg color

2 tablespoons fruit, vegetable, or spice per egg color (e.g., beet for pink, blueberries for dark blue, spinach for green, red cabbage for light blue, red wine for purple)

FOR THE EGG WASH

1 large egg

⅛ teaspoon water

1. **MAKE THE STARTER:** About 8 to 12 hours before mixing your dough, combine the starter or yeast, sugar, water, and flour in a clean container. Cover and leave at room temperature. It will increase in volume and become a very thick, aerated dough.

2. **WARM THE MILK:** Heat the milk until it reaches a temperature of 115°F to 120°F.

CONTINUED ON NEXT PAGE

3. **WEIGH THE INGREDIENTS:** Tare the bowl and combine 115 grams of warm milk, 55 grams of warm water, the instant yeast, and the sugar. Add 150 grams of the starter, then add the flour.

4. **MIX:** Mix the ingredients together until a shaggy dough is formed, then add the eggs and the slightly warm melted butter. Mix to combine, then add the salt, the remaining 10 grams of water, and the lemon zest. Mix well.

5. **KNEAD:** Turn the dough out onto a work surface and knead for 10 to 15 minutes by hand or 3 to 8 minutes on low in a stand mixer, until the dough is smooth, is no longer sticky, and releases easily from the bowl or work surface.

6. **BULK FERMENT:** Cover the dough and allow to ferment for 1½ to 2 hours, until doubled in volume.

7. **DYE THE EGGS:** While the dough is fermenting, dye the eggs. For naturally dyed eggs, bring the water to a boil, then add the salt, vinegar, and a fruit, vegetable, or spice for coloring. Reduce the heat to a simmer for 30 minutes, then strain the mixture and place in a bowl to cool. Repeat to create additional colors. Once the dyed water is no longer hot, add 4 to 5 uncooked eggs to the bowl and let them soak in the color(s) until they are dyed the desired hue. Wipe the dyed eggs clean and set aside.

8. **PREPARE THE BAKING SHEET:** Place a large sheet of parchment on a flat baking sheet.

9. **DIVIDE THE DOUGH:** Place the dough on a lightly floured work surface. Divide the dough into 3 equal pieces.

10. **SHAPE:** Roll each piece of dough until it is about 24 inches long. Braid the three ropes together, then bring the ends of each rope together and pinch to form a braided wreath. Take the dyed eggs and tuck them deeply into the strands of the bread, evenly spaced around the wreath. Place a cup in the center to prevent the dough from expanding and closing off the wreath center as it proofs.

11. **PROOF:** Cover and proof for 45 to 75 minutes, until the bread is about 1½ times larger in volume. Touching the dough with a fingertip should leave an indentation. Remove the cup from the center of the loaf.

12. **PREHEAT:** Preheat the oven to 350°F.

13. **EGG WASH:** Prepare the egg wash and brush all over the bread and into the crevices of the braid. Avoid getting egg wash on the dyed eggs.

14. **BAKE:** Place the baking sheet in the oven and spray the walls of the oven with water to create steam. Bake for 25 to 30 minutes, until the outside is golden brown and the inner part of the ring is baked.

15. **COOL:** Allow the bread to cool for at least 30 minutes.

16. **SERVING:** Cut the bread into slices and serve.

CHEESE-HERB BABKA

Yield: 1 large shaped bread (serves 10 to 12)

PREP TIME: 40 TO 55 MINUTES | **INACTIVE TIME:** 13 TO 20 HOURS | **BAKE TIME:** 40 TO 50 MINUTES

TOOLS NEEDED: food scale, small pot, large bowl, spoon, plastic dough scraper, parchment paper, loaf pan, rolling pin, serrated bread knife

---

The fresh flavors of a spring herb garden and the blend of cheeses create a bread ready for a spring brunch with friends or a weekend dinner with family.

FOR THE STARTER

15 grams sourdough starter (1 tablespoon) or ⅛ teaspoon instant yeast

110 grams water (½ cup)

110 grams all-purpose flour (¾ cup)

FOR THE DOUGH

130 grams milk (5 tablespoons)

70 grams warm water, divided (¼ cup plus 3½ tablespoons)

5 grams white cane sugar (1 teaspoon)

3 grams instant yeast (1 teaspoon) (may be omitted—see Focaccia Picnic Sandwiches tips on page 55)

28 grams unsalted butter, at room temperature or melted (2 tablespoons)

200 grams starter (1 cup)

340 grams all-purpose flour (2¼ cups plus 3 tablespoons)

40 grams whole-wheat flour (¼ cup)

8 grams salt (1½ teaspoons)

FOR THE FILLING

30 grams unsalted butter, at room temperature (2 tablespoons)

125 grams mozzarella cheese, grated, plus more for topping (1½ cups, loosely filled)

25 grams Parmesan cheese, freshly grated, plus more for topping (½ cup, loosely filled)

6 grams fresh chives, minced (2 tablespoons)

2 grams fresh rosemary, minced (1 teaspoon)

2 grams fresh Italian flat-leaf parsley, minced (1 teaspoon)

1. **MAKE THE STARTER:** About 8 to 12 hours before mixing your dough, combine the starter or yeast, water, and flour in a bowl. Mix well, cover, and leave at room temperature to allow the yeast to activate. It will become bubbly and double in volume.

2. **WARM THE MILK:** Heat the milk until it reaches a temperature of 115°F to 120°F.

3. **WEIGH THE INGREDIENTS:** Making sure to tare your mixing bowl on the scale after each addition, combine 110 grams of warm milk, 60 grams of warm water, the sugar, and the instant yeast. Allow the yeast to dissolve. Add the butter, 200 grams of starter, the all-purpose flour, and the whole-wheat flour.

4. **MIX:** Mix the ingredients together until a shaggy dough is formed, then add the salt and the remaining 10 grams of water. Mix to combine.

CONTINUED ON NEXT PAGE

5. **KNEAD:** Turn the dough out and knead for 10 to 15 minutes by hand or 3 to 8 minutes on low speed in a stand mixer, until the dough is smooth, is no longer sticky, and releases easily from the bowl or work surface.

6. **BULK FERMENT:** Cover the dough and allow to ferment for 1½ to 2 hours, until doubled in volume.

7. **PREPARE THE LOAF PAN:** Line a loaf pan with parchment paper and set aside. (See step 6 of Zucchini Spice Quick Bread on page 44.)

8. **SHAPE:** On a lightly floured work surface, roll the dough with a rolling pin into an 11-by-18-inch rectangle. Spread the butter over the dough with a spatula until completely covered. Evenly sprinkle the mozzarella and Parmesan cheeses over the butter, then sprinkle the chives, rosemary, and parsley evenly over the cheeses. Starting at the short end, roll the dough up into a log. The final rolled dough will have lots of spiraled layers and will be 11 inches wide. Use a bread knife to cut through the log from end to end, splitting it in half longways. The lines of rolled dough, cheese, and herbs will show inside the cut. Carefully intertwine the two pieces two or three times, making sure that the layers of dough, cheese, and herbs face up. Handle the dough gently to help prevent the cheese and herbs from falling out. Carefully transfer the twisted dough into the parchment paper–lined loaf pan with the exposed layers facing up. Add extra mozzarella and Parmesan cheese to the top, if desired.

9. **PROOF:** Cover and proof in a warm place for 45 to 60 minutes, until the layers appear puffy.

10. **PREHEAT:** Preheat the oven to 350°F.

11. **BAKE:** Place the proofed babka in the preheated oven. Bake for 40 to 50 minutes, until the cheese is melted and the top has a golden, toasted look.

12. **COOL:** Let cool for at least 20 minutes.

TIP: Fresh herbs can be substituted depending on preference and availability.

HOT CROSS BRAIDED WREATH

Yield: 1 large shaped bread (serves 8 or more)

PREP TIME: 40 TO 45 MINUTES | **INACTIVE TIME:** 11 TO 16 HOURS | **BAKE TIME:** 25 TO 30 MINUTES

TOOLS NEEDED: small pot, food scale, large bowl, spoon, plastic dough scraper, zester, parchment paper, baking sheet, pastry brush, spray bottle, whisk, piping bag or zip-top bag

A twist on hot cross buns, this braid looks beautiful and is filled with the traditional sweet and spiced flavors. This hot cross braided wreath comes together easily for a sweet way to celebrate Passion Week, Good Friday, or Easter Sunday.

FOR THE STARTER

30 grams sourdough starter (2 tablespoons) or ⅛ teaspoon instant yeast

15 grams white cane sugar (1 tablespoon)

50 grams water (3½ tablespoons)

100 grams all-purpose flour (⅔ cup)

FOR THE DOUGH

200 grams milk (¾ cup plus ½ tablespoon)

3 grams instant yeast (1 teaspoon)

150 grams starter (about ¾ cup)

42 grams butter, at room temperature or melted (3 tablespoons)

60 grams brown sugar (⅓ cup)

400 grams bread flour (2¾ cups plus 1 tablespoon)

100 grams whole-wheat flour (¾ cup)

90 grams freshly squeezed orange juice (⅓ cup, from about 1 medium orange)

9 grams salt (1½ teaspoons)

1 large egg

2 grams ground cinnamon (½ teaspoon)

1 gram ground nutmeg (¼ teaspoon)

1 gram ground cloves (⅛ teaspoon)

Zest of 1 orange

Zest of 1 lemon

20 grams water (1 tablespoon)

30 grams raisins (3 tablespoons)

60 grams dried sweetened cranberries, roughly chopped (⅓ cup)

FOR THE EGG WASH

1 large egg

⅛ teaspoon water

FOR THE VANILLA ICING

130 grams powdered sugar (about 1 cup)

¼ teaspoon vanilla extract

1 to 3 teaspoons milk or freshly squeezed orange juice

1. **MAKE THE STARTER:** About 8 to 12 hours before mixing your dough, combine the starter or yeast, sugar, water, and flour in a bowl. Mix well, cover, and leave at room temperature to allow the yeast to activate. It will double in volume.

2. **WARM THE MILK:** Heat the milk until it reaches a temperature of 115°F to 120°F.

3. **WEIGH THE INGREDIENTS:** Making sure to tare your mixing bowl on the scale after each addition, combine 180 grams of the warm milk, the instant yeast, and 150 grams of the starter. Add the butter, brown sugar, bread flour, and whole-wheat flour.

4. **MIX:** Mix the ingredients together until a shaggy dough is formed, then add the orange juice, salt, egg, cinnamon, nutmeg, cloves, orange zest, lemon zest, and water. Mix together to combine, then fold in the raisins and cranberries.

5. **KNEAD:** Turn the dough out onto a work surface and knead for 10 to 15 minutes by hand or 4 to 8 minutes on low speed in a stand mixer, until the dough is smooth, is no longer sticky, and releases easily from the bowl or work surface.

6. **BULK FERMENT:** Cover the dough and allow it to ferment for 1½ to 2 hours, until doubled in volume.

7. **PREPARE THE BAKING SHEET:** Line a baking sheet with parchment paper and set aside.

8. **SHAPE:** Divide the dough into 3 equal pieces. Roll each piece of dough into a 24-inch-long rope. Braid the ropes together, then bring the ends of each rope together and pinch to form a braided wreath. Place a cup in the center of the wreath to prevent the dough from expanding and closing off the center of the wreath.

9. **PROOF:** Cover and proof in a warm place for 45 to 60 minutes, until the dough has nearly doubled in size.

10. **PREHEAT:** Preheat the oven to 350°F.

11. **EGG WASH:** Prepare the egg wash by beating together the egg and water and brush the mixture all over the wreath and inside the crevices of the braids.

12. **BAKE:** Place the braided loaf in the preheated oven. Spray the oven walls with water to create steam, then immediately close the door to trap it inside. Bake for 25 to 30 minutes. The outside of the wreath should be golden brown and should be fully baked on the inside of the ring.

13. **COOL:** Allow the bread to cool for about 30 minutes before icing, or serve un-iced for a simpler presentation.

14. **PREPARE THE VANILLA ICING:** Sift the powdered sugar into a bowl, then add the vanilla and milk. Whisk until smooth and thick. Place the icing in a pastry bag with a thin round tip (or a plastic ziptop bag with a very small corner snipped off). For a more traditional look, pipe a cross at the top of the wreath, then decorate the rest with zig-zag piping. Or pipe zig-zag icing around the entire wreath.

TIPS: Instant yeast can be omitted to create a naturally fermented bread. The dough will take 2 to 3 times longer during the fermentation and proofing processes.
The lemon zest can be replaced with additional orange zest. The dried cranberries can be substituted for raisins and vice versa.

KULICH EASTER BREAD
(PASKA)

Yield: 3 large loaves

PREP TIME: 60 TO 95 MINUTES | **INACTIVE TIME:** 11 TO 15 HOURS | **BAKE TIME:** 30 TO 35 MINUTES

TOOLS NEEDED: 3 large paper panettone paper molds (5- to 7-inch diameter), food scale, small pot, extra-large mixing bowl, spoon, zester, whisk, plastic dough scraper, large baking tray, spray bottle

This bread is called kulich in Russia and is also known as paska in Ukraine. Often served for Orthodox Easter, it is a tall, sweet, eggy bread with a very soft irregular crumb similar to angel food cake or panettone.

FOR THE STARTER
30 grams active sourdough starter (2 tablespoons) or ⅛ teaspoon instant yeast

30 grams white cane sugar (2 tablespoons)

100 grams water (7 tablespoons)

200 grams bread flour (1⅓ cups)

FOR THE FIRST DOUGH
350 grams milk (1 cup plus 7 tablespoons)

9 grams instant yeast (1 tablespoon)

300 grams starter (1½ cups)

6 large eggs, whisked

225 grams full-fat sour cream (¾ cup plus 1 tablespoon)

660 grams bread flour (4¼ cups plus 2½ tablespoons)

210 grams white cane sugar (1 cup plus 2 teaspoons)

Zest of 1 lemon

FOR THE FINAL DOUGH
345 grams bread flour (2¼ cups plus ½ tablespoon)

9 grams salt (1½ teaspoons)

10 grams water (2 teaspoons)

168 grams unsalted butter, melted (¾ cup)

90 grams raisins (½ cup plus 1 tablespoon)

FOR THE LEMON GLAZE
260 grams powdered sugar (about 2 cups)

2 to 4 tablespoons freshly squeezed lemon juice

1 to 2 tablespoons rainbow sprinkles (optional)

1. **MAKE THE STARTER:** About 8 to 12 hours before mixing your dough, combine the starter or yeast, sugar, water, and flour in a clean container. Cover and leave at room temperature until increased in volume and bubbly. (If using sourdough starter, starting with a recently refreshed, active starter will create better activity in the starter made for this recipe.)

2. **WARM THE MILK:** Heat the milk until it reaches a temperature of 115°F to 120°F.

3. **WEIGH THE INGREDIENTS:** Making sure to tare your mixing bowl on the scale after each addition, combine 330 grams of warm milk, the instant yeast, and 300 grams of starter. Stir the mixture together to begin breaking the starter apart and dissolving the yeast.

4. **WHISK THE EGGS:** In a separate bowl, whisk the eggs. Add the sour cream and whisk together. Set aside.

5. **MIX:** Tare the milk and starter mixture. Add the bread flour and stir until it begins absorbing the liquid. Add the egg and sour cream mixture. Mix well, folding by hand for 5 to 10 minutes or in a stand mixer with a dough hook for 3 to 6 minutes, until the dough is soft and has come together.

6. **ADD THE SUGAR:** Slowly add the sugar, 10 grams at a time, folding it in until fully incorporated. Add the lemon zest and continue to fold until the dough is smooth.

7. **FIRST RISE:** Cover the dough and leave at room temperature to grow and become bubbly for 1 to 2 hours.

8. **MIX THE FINAL DOUGH:** Tare the bowl holding the first dough, then add the bread flour, salt, and water. Fold by hand for 4 to 8 minutes or in a stand mixer for 3 to 6 minutes, until the flour is incorporated and the dough is elastic.

9. **ADD THE BUTTER:** Slowly add the slightly warm melted butter one-quarter at a time. Fold in each addition until absorbed. Fold until it's strong, elastic, and smooth.

10. **ADD THE RAISINS:** Fold in the raisins.

11. **SECOND RISE:** Cover the dough and allow it to ferment at room temperature for 2½ to 3½ hours, until the dough has doubled in volume.

12. **FILL THE MOLDS:** Arrange the three panettone paper molds on a large baking tray. Divide the dough as equally as possible into the three molds, without pressing air out of the dough or pushing it down.

13. **PROOF:** Cover each mold with a piece of plastic wrap. Leave at room temperature for 1½ to 2 hours, until the dough has risen to 1 to 2 inches below the rim of the molds. Touching the dough with your fingertip should leave a slight indentation.

14. **PREHEAT:** Preheat the oven to 350°F. Rearrange the oven racks so that the tall molds can fit in the center of the oven.

15. **BAKE:** Place the filled molds in the oven, spray the oven walls with water, and close the door. Bake for 30 to 35 minutes, until the breads have a golden-brown top and the inside is baked (it should reach an internal temperature of 200°F).

16. **COOL:** Allow the bread to cool for 30 to 60 minutes, or until it reaches room temperature, before glazing. Remove the paper mold by carefully ripping sections away from the outside of the bread.

17. **MAKE THE GLAZE:** Whisk together the powdered sugar and lemon juice until it reaches a good consistency for drizzling. Using a spoon, generously pour the icing over the breads. Cover the top and let the glaze drip down the sides. Add sprinkles.

18. **SERVE:** Cut into wedges or slice and serve.

Rosemary-Tomato Focaccia, page 62

Chapter Three

SUMMER

*Fresh flavors, cold sandwiches, picnics, and outdoor cooking
come to mind for summer meals. In summer, you can often
find my family grilling food by a swimming pool or lingering
over a table outside long after dinner has ended.
Use seasonal summer produce, like fresh berries in Berry Scones
or garden zucchini in Zucchini Spice Quick Bread. For your next
summer barbecue, make Potato Burger Buns or Grilled Pizzas.*

BERRY SCONES

Yield: 12 scones

PREP TIME: 25 MINUTES | **INACTIVE TIME:** 30 TO 40 MINUTES | **BAKE TIME:** 18 TO 20 MINUTES

TOOLS NEEDED: pie dish, parchment paper, 2 baking sheets, food scale, large bowl, spoon, zester, knife, pastry cutter or 2 forks, whisk, small bowl

---

I love a flaky, buttery scone, especially one filled with seasonal summer berries. We frequently enjoy these as a weekend treat, but they're also great for brunch, bridal showers, or baby showers. The key to a flaky scone is keeping the butter very cold and not overmixing the dough.

FOR THE DOUGH

150 grams berries, such as blueberries, blackberries, or combination, divided (1 cup)

400 grams all-purpose flour (2½ cups)

200 grams white cane sugar, plus more for topping (1 cup)

15 grams baking powder (1 tablespoon)

4 grams salt (½ teaspoon)

Zest of 1 lemon

226 grams unsalted butter, cold (1 cup)

200 grams whole milk, chilled (¾ cup)

FOR THE GLAZE

65 grams powdered sugar (about ½ cup)

1 to 3 teaspoons freshly squeezed lemon juice

1. **PREPARE THE PIE DISH AND THE FROZEN BERRIES:** Line a pie dish with parchment paper and fill with 10 to 20 berries. Place the pie dish in the freezer.

2. **PREPARE THE BAKING SHEETS:** Line two baking sheets with parchment paper and set aside.

3. **WEIGH THE INGREDIENTS:** Making sure to tare your bowl on the scale after each addition, combine the flour, sugar, baking powder, salt, and lemon zest. Stir.

4. **ADD THE BUTTER:** Cut the cold butter in half, then cut each half into eight pieces and add to the dry mixture. With two forks or a pastry cutter, cut the butter into the flour mixture so that the smaller pieces distribute through the dough until crumbly and sandy. Some big pieces are okay, but aim for pieces no bigger than a pea.

5. **MIX:** Add the chilled milk and stir to combine, making sure not to overmix. Gently fold in the remaining berries until just incorporated.

6. **SHAPE:** Lightly flour the parchment papers. Place one-half of the dough on each sheet. Gently pat each half of the dough into a large circle that is about 1 inch thick. Take out the nearly frozen berries and press them into the top.

CONTINUED ON NEXT PAGE

7. **CHILL:** Cover the dough and place in the refrigerator to chill for 10 to 20 minutes, or freeze.

8. **PREHEAT:** Preheat the oven to 400°F.

9. **DIVIDE:** Cut each circle of dough into 6 wedges (like a pizza). Carefully spread the scones out on the baking sheets, making sure they are at least 2 inches apart.

10. **BAKE:** Place the baking sheets in the oven and bake for 18 to 20 minutes, until the scones are golden brown on the edges and a toothpick inserted in the thickest part of each scone comes out clean.

11. **COOL:** Allow the scones to cool at room temperature for about 20 minutes.

12. **GLAZE AND SERVE:** Whisk together the powdered sugar and lemon juice until it reaches a good consistency for drizzling. Drizzle the glaze over the cooled scones and serve.

TIP: Blueberries, blackberries, olallieberries, and boysenberries all work well for this recipe. Frozen berries may be used instead of fresh.

ZUCCHINI SPICE QUICK BREAD

Yield: 2 large loaves

PREP TIME: 25 MINUTES | **INACTIVE TIME:** 20 MINUTES | **BAKE TIME:** 50 TO 55 MINUTES

TOOLS NEEDED: cheese grater, fine-mesh strainer, food scale, 2 large bowls, spoon, pan or small pot, food scale, scissors, parchment paper, 2 loaf pans, spatula

---

My picky son absolutely loves this zucchini spice quick bread! We like to have this bread as a special breakfast with coffee. The zucchini gives this bread an incredibly moist bite, combined with a sweet and spicy flavor that everyone will love.

---

2 zucchini

3 large eggs

100 grams brown sugar (½ cup)

100 grams white cane sugar, plus more for topping (½ cup)

4 grams vanilla extract (1 teaspoon)

6 grams salt (1 teaspoon)

210 grams whole-wheat flour (1½ cups)

210 grams all-purpose flour (1½ cups)

4 grams baking powder (1 teaspoon)

5 grams baking soda (1 teaspoon)

6 grams ground cinnamon (2 teaspoons)

2 grams ground ginger (½ teaspoon)

2 grams ground nutmeg (½ teaspoon)

1 gram ground cloves (¼ teaspoon)

113 grams unsalted butter, melted (½ cup)

1. **PREHEAT:** Preheat the oven to 350°F.

2. **GRATE THE ZUCCHINI:** Grate the zucchini into coarse pieces using a cheese grater. Place the zucchini in a fine mesh strainer propped over a bowl to allow excess water to drain.

3. **MIX THE WET INGREDIENTS:** Place a large mixing bowl on the scale. Tare the bowl, then add the eggs, brown sugar, cane sugar, vanilla, and salt. Beat the ingredients together. Set aside.

4. **MIX THE DRY INGREDIENTS:** Tare a separate bowl, then add the whole-wheat flour, all-purpose flour, baking powder, baking soda, cinnamon, ginger, nutmeg, and cloves. Pour the dry mixture into the wet mixture. Stir to combine.

5. **ADD THE ZUCCHINI AND BUTTER:** Add the grated and drained zucchini to the batter. (There should be about 400 grams.) Add the melted butter and stir until combined.

CONTINUED ON NEXT PAGE

6. **PREPARE THE LOAF PANS:** Cut two square pieces of parchment, at least 12-by-12 inches. Turn a loaf pan over and center the two parchment squares over the bottom of the pan. Use scissors to make four cuts from the edge of the paper to each corner. Turn the pan back over and use the cut slits to fold the edges of the parchment paper in to fit snugly into the corners of the pan. One piece of parchment paper goes into each loaf pan.

7. **FILL THE LOAF PANS:** Use a spatula to pour the dough equally between the loaf pans. For an extra crispiness on top, sprinkle 1 to 2 tablespoons of sugar on top of the loaves.

8. **BAKE:** Place the pans in the oven and bake for 50 to 55 minutes. The bread should be golden brown on top, and a knife inserted into the center should come out clean.

9. **COOL:** Allow the loaves to cool for about 20 minutes before slicing.

TIP: Tie a ribbon around the loaf with a gift tag for a perfect homemade present for a friend or neighbor.

CIABATTA SANDWICH ROLLS

Yield: 8 rolls

PREP TIME: 30 TO 40 MINUTES | **INACTIVE TIME:** 3 TO 4 HOURS | **BAKE TIME:** 15 TO 20 MINUTES

TOOLS NEEDED: food scale, large bowl, spoon, plastic dough scraper, parchment paper, baking stone or flat baking sheet, steam pan, spray bottle, cooling rack

Ciabatta's soft, chewy center and thin, crispy crust make it the perfect sandwich base. Enjoy these ciabatta sandwich rolls filled with your favorite sandwich fixings or serve them at a build-your-own-sandwich buffet for a summer party.

400 grams warm water, divided (1⅔ cups plus ½ tablespoon)

2 grams instant yeast (½ teaspoon)

500 grams bread flour (3½ cups)

10 grams sea salt (1½ teaspoons)

1. **WEIGH THE INGREDIENTS:** Making sure to tare your mixing bowl after each addition, combine 390 grams of warm water and the yeast and allow it to dissolve. Add the bread flour.

2. **MIX:** Using a spoon or dough hook in a stand mixer, mix all the ingredients together until a shaggy dough is formed. Be sure to scrape the sides of the bowl so that no dry pieces of dough stick to it.

3. **ADD SALT:** Tare the bowl. Pour in the salt, then add the remaining 10 grams of water to dissolve the salt.

4. **STRETCH AND FOLD:** Fold the dough by hand for 8 to 12 minutes or with a dough hook in a stand mixer for 4 to 8 minutes, until the dough no longer sticks to the sides of the bowl and pulls away easily.

5. **BULK FERMENT:** Cover the dough and leave it in a warm place to ferment for 1½ to 2 hours, until doubled in volume.

6. **DIVIDE THE DOUGH:** Cut an extra-long sheet of parchment (if using pre-cut sheets, slightly overlap two sheets) and generously flour them. Pour the ciabatta dough onto the floured surface. Doing your best not to release any of the built-up air, use the sharp edge of a dough scraper coated in flour to divide the dough. This dough is difficult to weigh due to its high hydration, so to divide, cut the dough in half, then cut each piece in half again. Finally, cut each piece in half again, resulting in eight pieces. Gently push the pieces of dough so that they are evenly spaced from each other, 3 to 4 inches apart.

CONTINUED ON NEXT PAGE

7. **SHAPE THE DOUGH:** Flour your hands and the dough scraper. With the scraper, gently push a piece of dough by the edges to move it into position on the parchment and shape. Alternate which sides you push, gently forming a rough rectangle that measures 3½-by-4½ inches. Repeat with the remaining dough. The rolls will not look identical, but aim for them all to be a similar size. Dust the tops with flour and cover them with a clean, dry kitchen cloth.

8. **PROOF:** Proof the rolls for 45 minutes to 1½ hours.

9. **PREHEAT:** About 30 minutes before the proofing is finished, place a baking stone on the center rack of the oven (bake directly on a baking sheet if you do not have a baking stone) with a steam pan filled with water on the bottom rack and preheat the oven to 500°F.

10. **BAKE:** Cut the parchment sheet in the middle to bake the ciabatta in two batches. Transfer one sheet of parchment with four proofed ciabatta rolls into the hot oven. Spray a generous mist of water on the oven walls and close the door. Reduce the heat to 460°F and bake for 10 minutes, then remove the steam pan and bake for 5 to 10 more minutes, until the crust is crisp and golden brown. Return the steam pan to the oven and repeat this step with the other batch of ciabatta rolls.

11. **COOL:** Cool the rolls on a cooling rack for at least 30 minutes.

TIP: To add more depth to the flavor of these rolls, the dough can be left in the refrigerator to ferment for up to 2 days. Let the dough come to room temperature before dividing and shaping.

GRILLED PIZZAS

Yield: 8 small pizzas

PREP TIME: 40 TO 65 MINUTES | **INACTIVE TIME:** 2 TO 3 HOURS
BAKE TIME: 2 TO 3 MINUTES PER PIZZA

TOOLS NEEDED: food scale, large bowl, spoon, plastic dough scraper, barbecue grill (or standard oven—see tips), rolling pin, parchment paper, 2 baking sheets, small bowl, grill-safe oil/marinade brush, timer, metal spatula, pizza cutter or large knife

The benefits of making grilled pizzas is twofold: They are a delicious and different take on an old favorite food, and they can be made in the hot summer weather without heating your house up by turning on the oven.

FOR THE DOUGH

300 grams warm water, divided (1¼ cups plus 1 teaspoon)

2 grams instant yeast (½ teaspoon)

6 grams white cane sugar (1 teaspoon)

450 grams bread flour (3 cups plus 3½ tablespoons)

50 grams whole-wheat flour (⅓ cup)

10 grams sea salt (1½ teaspoons)

FOR THE GRILL

½ cup oil with high smoke point (e.g., avocado, ghee, vegetable)

FOR THE TOPPINGS

¼ to ½ cup pizza sauce

16 ounces low-moisture mozzarella cheese, shredded

4 ounces pepperoni

2 ounces Parmesan cheese, freshly grated

2 teaspoons oregano, dried

1. **WEIGH THE INGREDIENTS:** Making sure to tare your mixing bowl after each addition, combine 290 grams of water, the yeast, and the sugar. Allow the yeast to dissolve, then add the bread flour and whole-wheat flour.

2. **MIX:** Using a spoon or dough hook in a stand mixer, mix together until a shaggy dough forms.

3. **ADD THE SALT:** Tare the bowl. Pour in the salt. Add the remaining 10 grams of water on top of the salt to dissolve. Mix to combine.

4. **KNEAD:** Knead the dough by hand for 8 to 12 minutes or with a dough hook in a stand mixer for 4 to 8 minutes, until the dough no longer sticks to the sides of the bowl and pulls away easily.

5. **BULK FERMENT:** Cover the dough and leave it in a warm place to ferment for 1½ to 2 hours, until doubled in volume.

6. **PREHEAT THE GRILL:** Preheat the grill until it is a steady 500°F. (Note: Once baking starts, the grill will not stay at 500°F and would be too hot if kept at that temperature. You will be aiming to maintain a range of 350°F to 400°F while baking—400°F is optimal.)

CONTINUED ON NEXT PAGE

7. **DIVIDE THE DOUGH:** Turn the dough out onto a work surface and divide into 8 pieces (about 100 grams each). Roll each piece into a ball. Cover the dough balls with a cloth.

8. **PREP THE GRILL TRANSFER TOOLS:** Cut two large squares of parchment paper and place each on a baking sheet. Put the high-heat oil in a bowl and get a grill marinade brush ready (an alternative would be a spray bottle made for cooking oil).

9. **ROLL THE DOUGH:** Lightly flour your work surface. Roll each ball of dough until it is a 7- to 8-inch-wide circle. Place the discs of rolled dough on the parchment sheets.

10. **PREBAKE THE PIZZA CRUSTS:** Once the grill is at temperature and the ingredients are all prepared, brush the oil (prepared in step 8) on the tops of the rolled-out pizza crusts and grill grates. Place 2 or 3 crusts on the grill, oil-side down. Close the grill lid and grill for 30 seconds. Open the lid, quickly brush the tops of the dough with the oil, and flip them using a metal spatula. Close the grill lid again and cook for 30 more seconds. Open the lid and transfer the pizza crusts back onto the parchment paper–lined baking sheet. Repeat with the rest of the pizza dough.

11. **TOP THE PIZZAS:** Once all the crusts have prebaked, top them with the pizza sauce and other toppings as desired. For a flavorful pepperoni pizza, top with about 1 tablespoon of pizza sauce, 2 to 3 tablespoons of mozzarella, 2 to 4 pepperoni slices, a generous sprinkling of Parmesan, and ¼ teaspoon of oregano.

12. **BAKE:** Place 2 or 3 topped pizzas on the grill, close the lid, and bake for 1 minute. Keep an eye on the bottoms of the crusts to avoid burning. Open the lid, remove the pizzas, and repeat.

13. **COOL:** Allow the pizzas to cool for 5 to 15 minutes before slicing.

TIP: To make these pizzas in the oven, preheat a baking stone (or an insulated baking sheet) to 550°F. Add the toppings to the pizzas and bake for 5 to 8 minutes.

POTATO BURGER BUNS

Yield: 8 large hamburger buns

PREP TIME: 40 TO 60 MINUTES | **INACTIVE TIME:** 2½ TO 3½ HOURS | **BAKE TIME:** 20 TO 24 MINUTES

TOOLS NEEDED: food scale, potato peeler, knife, large pot, colander, 2 large
bowls, spoon, small pot, parchment paper, 2 baking sheets, plastic dough
scraper, plastic wrap, small bowl, pastry brush, spray bottle

---

*These burger buns are easy to make and stay super soft. These bake up
beautifully into large, full buns that are perfect for a summer barbecue burger!*

FOR THE DOUGH

300 grams potato, peeled, cooked, and mashed (about 1 cup after mashing, from 2 medium to large potatoes)

120 grams milk (¼ cup plus 3 tablespoons)

100 grams warm water, divided (¼ cup plus 3 tablespoons)

68 grams unsalted butter, at room temperature (¼ cup)

15 grams brown sugar (1 tablespoon)

6 grams instant yeast (2 teaspoons)

450 grams bread flour (3 cups)

50 grams whole-wheat flour (⅓ cup)

10 grams salt (1½ teaspoons)

2 large eggs

FOR THE EGG WASH

1 large egg

½ teaspoon water

Pinch salt

1 tablespoon poppy seeds or sesame seeds (optional)

1. **COOK THE POTATOES:** Peel and quarter the potatoes. Bring a large pot of water to a boil. Add the potatoes and reduce the heat to medium or medium-low to simmer. Cover and cook for 20 to 25 minutes, until the potatoes are fork-tender. Once the potatoes are finished cooking, immediately strain them using a colander, then run them under cool water to stop further cooking.

2. **MASH THE POTATOES:** Put the cooked potatoes in a mixing bowl and mash until smooth. If using an electric mixer, mash the potatoes using the paddle mixing tool until there are almost no lumps—don't overwhip the potatoes or they will become too starchy. Set aside.

3. **WARM THE MILK:** Heat the milk until it reaches a temperature of 115°F to 120°F.

4. **WEIGH THE INGREDIENTS:** Tare a separate large mixing bowl, then combine 300 grams of mashed potatoes, 100 grams of warm milk, 90 grams of water, and the butter. Add the sugar and instant yeast; allow the sugar to dissolve. Finally, add the bread flour and whole-wheat flour.

5. **MIX:** Mix the ingredients together until a shaggy dough forms, then add the salt, the

CONTINUED ON NEXT PAGE

remaining 10 grams of water, and the eggs. Mix to combine.

6. **FOLD:** Stretch and fold the dough by hand for 10 to 15 minutes or 5 to 10 minutes using a dough hook in a stand mixer, until the dough no longer sticks to the sides of the bowl and pulls away easily.

7. **BULK FERMENT:** Cover the dough and allow it to ferment for 1½ to 2 hours, until doubled in volume.

8. **PREPARE THE BAKING SHEETS:** Place two large pieces of parchment paper on two flat baking sheets.

9. **DIVIDE:** Turn the dough out onto a floured work surface. Divide the dough into 8 equal pieces (about 163 grams each).

10. **SHAPE:** This dough is very soft and can be difficult to shape. Use a floured surface and a dough scraper to fold the bottom of the dough over the top. Then rotate, using the dough scraper to maneuver the dough in a circular motion, tightening it into a smooth, taut ball. Gently pick up the bun and place it on one of the prepared baking sheets. Repeat with the rest of the dough. There should be four buns on each baking sheet.

11. **PROOF:** Cover the shaped buns with plastic wrap or a cloth and proof for 30 to 60 minutes, until the rolls are puffy and at least 1½ times larger.

12. **PREHEAT:** Preheat the oven to 375°F.

13. **MAKE THE EGG WASH:** Beat together the egg, water, and salt in a small bowl or cup. Use a pastry brush to brush the egg wash all over the tops of the buns. Sprinkle on ¼ to ½ teaspoon of poppy seeds.

14. **BAKE:** Place the baking sheets with proofed rolls into the preheated oven, spray the walls of the oven with water, and close the door to trap the steam. Bake for 20 to 24 minutes, until the rolls are golden brown on top.

15. **COOL:** Let the rolls cool for at least 30 minutes before serving.

TIP: For faster potato prep, use the microwave. Prepare the potatoes as directed, then add to a glass bowl with 1 tablespoon of water and cover with plastic wrap. Microwave on high for 8 to 10 minutes, until fork-tender, then leave to cool for 5 to 10 minutes.

BLUEBERRY-LEMON SOURDOUGH COUNTRY BREAD

Yield: 1 loaf

PREP TIME: 35 TO 40 MINUTES | **INACTIVE TIME:** 13½ TO 20 HOURS | **BAKE TIME:** 40 MINUTES

TOOLS NEEDED: food scale, food container, large bowl, spoon, zester, plastic dough scraper, parchment paper, bread proofing bowl or colander lined with a kitchen towel, large Dutch oven or steam pan, bread lame or serrated bread knife, spray bottle, cooling rack

---

Berry picking has become a summer tradition for our family. Blueberry picking in the foothills of the Sierras is a hot, sticky, satisfying endeavor. Lemon complements blueberries perfectly in this bread.

FOR THE STARTER
15 grams sourdough starter (1 tablespoon) or ⅛ teaspoon instant yeast

60 grams water (¼ cup plus 3 tablespoons)

60 grams all-purpose flour (⅔ cup)

FOR THE DOUGH
325 grams water, divided (1⅓ cups plus 2 teaspoons)

80 grams active starter (½ cup)

100 grams whole-wheat flour (¾ cup)

300 grams bread flour (2 cups plus 2 tablespoons)

8 grams sea salt (1½ teaspoons)

Zest of 1 lemon (¼ to ½ teaspoon)

80 grams fresh blueberries (⅓ to ½ cup)

Rice flour or semolina, for dusting proofing bowl

1. **REFRESH THE STARTER:** About 6 to 10 hours before mixing your dough, place the sourdough starter in a clean container. Add the water and flour, stir well, and cover. Leave out at room temperature until it doubles in volume and becomes bubbly. (See tips for substituting instant yeast.)

2. **WEIGH THE INGREDIENTS:** Making sure to tare after each addition, combine 315 grams of water, 80 grams of active starter, the whole-wheat flour, and the bread flour in a large mixing bowl.

3. **MIX:** Using a spoon, mix all the ingredients together by hand or in a stand mixer until there are no dry spots of flour left.

4. **AUTOLYSE:** Cover the bowl and let the dough rest for 20 minutes.

5. **ADD THE SALT:** After the resting time is finished, place the bowl of dough on the scale and tare. Add the salt, then slowly pour the remaining 10 grams of water over the salt to dissolve. Massage the salt and water into the dough, rotating it and folding it to make sure it is fully mixed in. Continue folding for 3 to 5 minutes.

CONTINUED ON NEXT PAGE

6. **REST:** Cover the bowl and allow the dough to rest for 30 minutes.

7. **STRETCH AND FOLD:** Add the lemon zest and blueberries to the center of the dough. Take the dough in hand and, one-quarter at a time, pull the dough upward, then fold it back into the middle. Repeat with the other three quarters until the blueberries and lemon zest are well distributed throughout the dough.

8. **BULK FERMENT:** Allow the dough to ferment at room temperature for 3 to 6 hours, until doubled in volume.

9. **PRE-SHAPE AND BENCH REST:** Transfer the dough to an unfloured surface. Quickly push the straight edge of a dough scraper under one-half of the dough, then fold it over itself. Push the scraper under one side of the dough and rotate in a circular motion 3 to 5 times until it's a round shape. Leave the dough to rest for 20 minutes.

10. **PREPARE THE PROOFING BOWL:** Dust your proofing bowl generously with rice flour, making sure to coat the sides well.

11. **FINAL SHAPE:** Flour the top of your dough. Push the straight edge of the dough scraper under the dough. Guiding with your opposite hand, flip the dough onto its floured side. Pick up the left and right edges of the dough, gently stretch outward, then fold the edges into the middle. Pinch the edges together to seal the seam. Take the end of the dough below the seam and roll it onto itself in a spiral until it seals at the opposite end. The floured side should be facing up once again. Without flipping the dough over, use the scraper to rotate the dough in a circle until it tightens into a tight ball. Quickly push the scraper under the dough and lift with your opposite hand, then flip the dough into the proofing bowl. The floured side should be down, and the sticky side should be up. Cover.

12. **PROOF:** Proof for 1 to 2 hours at room temperature. To test when the proofing is completed, wet your finger and gently press the dough. If it rises back up, leaving a slight indentation, it is ready to bake.

13. **PREHEAT:** After 30 to 60 minutes of proofing, preheat your oven to 500°F with the Dutch oven inside on the center rack. Substitute with a metal pan filled halfway with water on the lowest rack of the oven if you are planning to bake your bread on a baking sheet.

14. **BAKE:** Center an extra-long sheet of parchment paper over the proofing bowl. Holding the paper over the bowl by grasping the edges of the bowl, flip it to turn the dough out onto the parchment paper. Use a bread lame to score the top of your dough about ¼ inch deep. Carefully pick up the edges of the parchment and transfer the dough into the preheated Dutch oven (or onto the baking sheet). Cover with the lid and place it back in the oven. Spray the walls of the oven with water and shut the door. Reduce the oven temperature to 460°F and bake for 20 minutes. After 20 minutes, carefully remove the bread from the Dutch oven and place it directly on the oven rack. (Remove the steam pan if using manual steam.) Reduce the heat to 450°F and bake for an additional 20 minutes to create a golden-brown crust.

15. **COOL:** Allow the bread to cool for 1 hour on a cooling rack before slicing.

TIP: To substitute commercial yeast for the sourdough starter, mix 60 grams of flour, 60 grams of water, and ⅛ teaspoon of instant yeast. Add 3 grams of additional instant yeast in step 2. Bulk ferment for 1½ to 3 hours and proof for 30 to 90 minutes.

FOCACCIA PICNIC SANDWICHES

Yield: 1 large loaf (makes about 16 small sandwiches)

PREP TIME: 35 TO 40 MINUTES | **INACTIVE TIME:** 8½ TO 14 HOURS
BAKE TIME: 25 TO 30 MINUTES, PLUS 8 TO 12 MINUTES

TOOLS NEEDED: food scale, large bowl, spoon, plastic dough scraper, parchment paper, steam pan, baking stone, bread peel or baking sheet, cooling rack, bread knife

These summer sandwiches can be served warm or chilled. The melted cheese helps them stay together, making them great for travel and picnics, as a meal to deliver to a new family, or as a housewarming gift for new neighbors.

FOR THE STARTER
15 grams sourdough starter (1 tablespoon) or ⅛ teaspoon instant yeast

60 grams water (¼ cup plus 3 tablespoons)

60 grams all-purpose flour (⅔ cup)

FOR THE DOUGH
370 grams warm water, divided (1½ cups plus 1 tablespoon)

15 grams white cane sugar or honey (1 tablespoon)

2 grams instant yeast (½ teaspoon)

100 grams starter (about ½ cup)

450 grams all-purpose flour (3 cups plus 3½ tablespoons)

50 grams whole-wheat flour (⅓ cup)

11 grams salt (1½ teaspoons)

40 grams olive oil, plus more for the pan (3½ tablespoons)

FOR THE TOP
20 to 30 grams olive oil or avocado oil (2 to 3 tablespoons)

10 to 15 grams coarse sea salt (1 to 2 teaspoons)

FOR THE FILLING
30 to 60 grams pesto (2 to 4 tablespoons)

125 grams mozzarella cheese, grated (1½ cups, loosely filled)

1 tomato, thinly sliced

1. **MAKE THE STARTER:** About 6 to 10 hours before mixing your dough, mix together the starter or yeast, water, and flour in a bowl. Cover and leave at room temperature until doubled in volume and bubbly.

2. **WEIGH THE INGREDIENTS:** Making sure to tare after each addition, combine 360 grams of warm water, the sugar, instant yeast, and starter in a large bowl. Let the sugar dissolve, then add the all-purpose flour and whole-wheat flour.

3. **MIX:** Stir the ingredients together until a shaggy dough forms. Add the salt and oil. Pour the remaining 10 grams of water over the salt to dissolve it. Mix to combine.

4. **FOLD:** Stretch and fold the dough by hand for 8 to 10 minutes or 3 to 8 minutes using a dough hook in a stand mixer, until the dough no longer sticks to the sides of the bowl and pulls away easily.

5. **BULK FERMENT:** Place the dough in a clean bowl, cover, and ferment for 1½ to 2 hours, until doubled in volume.

6. **SHAPE:** Spread about 1 tablespoon of oil (avocado or olive) on parchment paper with your fingertips. Place the dough on the oiled parchment, then gently spread it out with oiled fingertips into a 10-inch circle with uniform thickness. If the dough resists shaping, leave it to rest for 10 minutes.

7. **PROOF:** Proof for 30 to 60 minutes at room temperature.

8. **PREHEAT:** After 30 minutes of proofing, preheat the oven to 475°F with a steam pan filled with water on a lower rack and a baking stone on the center rack.

9. **TOP THE FOCACCIA:** Before baking, top the dough with the oil; use your fingertips to make dimples in the top of the dough. Sprinkle coarse salt on top to taste.

10. **BAKE:** Use a bread peel or baking sheet to transfer the focaccia and parchment onto the preheated baking stone. (Bake directly on a baking sheet if not using a stone.) Close the oven door and reduce the temperature to 450°F. Bake for 25 to 30 minutes, until golden brown. Remove the steam pan after 10 minutes.

11. **COOL:** Allow to cool for 30 to 60 minutes.

12. **PREHEAT:** Preheat the oven to 400°F.

13. **CUT THE BREAD:** Once the bread is cool enough to handle, cut into four large pieces. Turn each piece of bread onto its cut side and slice through the middle to divide the top from the bottom.

14. **ASSEMBLE THE SANDWICHES:** Place the four bottom pieces of cut focaccia on a large piece of aluminum foil. Spread half of the pesto on the bottom layer of focaccia bread. Add the mozzarella and tomato slices. Spread the rest of the pesto on the underside of the top pieces, place them on top, and wrap the aluminum foil around the sandwiches to seal.

15. **HEAT THE SANDWICHES:** Place the wrapped sandwiches in the oven for 8 to 12 minutes.

16. **FINISH SLICING THE SANDWICHES AND SERVE:** Remove the sandwiches from the oven and carefully unwrap. Cut the sandwiches into quarters so that there are 16 small sandwiches total. Serve.

TIP: Instant yeast can be omitted to create a naturally fermented bread if you are using sourdough starter. The fermentation and proofing stages of this recipe will be 2 to 3 times longer if using this method.

MARBLED RYE SANDWICH BREAD

Yield: 1 loaf

PREP TIME: 50 MINUTES | **INACTIVE TIME:** 14 TO 23 HOURS | **BAKE TIME:** 35 TO 40 MINUTES

TOOLS NEEDED: food scale, food container, small pot, 2 large bowls, spoon, plastic dough scraper, loaf pan, parchment paper, rolling pin, steam pan, spray bottle, cooling rack

Marbled rye has a distinct sour flavor that many people love, and it makes a great sandwich bread. This bread would be beautiful for a summer luncheon or picnic. Rye bread has a lower gluten content, so kneading is ineffective. Just make sure to mix the dough until well combined.

FOR THE STARTER
30 grams sourdough starter (2 tablespoons) or ⅛ teaspoon instant yeast

15 grams white cane sugar (1 tablespoon)

50 grams water (3½ tablespoons)

100 grams all-purpose flour (⅔ cup)

FOR THE DOUGH
120 grams milk (¼ cup plus 3 tablespoons)

205 grams warm water, divided (¾ cup plus 1¾ tablespoons)

150 grams starter (about ¾ cup)

200 grams rye flour (1⅓ cups)

300 grams all-purpose flour (2 cups)

30 grams molasses (2 tablespoons)

5 grams caraway seeds (2 teaspoons)

10 grams sea salt (1½ teaspoons)

10 grams cacao powder (1 tablespoon)

1. **MAKE THE STARTER:** About 8 to 12 hours before mixing your dough, combine the starter or yeast, sugar, water, and flour in a clean container. Cover and leave at room temperature. It will increase in volume and become bubbly.

2. **WARM THE MILK:** Heat the milk until it reaches a temperature of 115°F to 120°F.

3. **WEIGH THE INGREDIENTS:** Making sure to tare after each addition, combine 100 grams of warm milk, 190 grams of warm water, 150 grams of starter, the rye flour, all-purpose flour, molasses, and caraway seeds in a mixing bowl.

4. **MIX:** Mix the ingredients together until a shaggy dough forms, then add the salt. Add the remaining 10 grams of water to dissolve the salt. Mix until well combined, being careful not to overmix.

5. **DIVIDE THE DOUGH:** Divide the dough in half (about 512 grams per half). Place one half in a separate bowl and cover.

6. **MIX IN THE CACAO POWDER:** Add the cacao powder and the remaining 5 grams of water to the remaining half of the dough. Mix well until all the cacao powder is incorporated into the dough to create a darker-hued dough, then cover.

7. **BULK FERMENT:** Ferment both bowls of dough in a warm place for 3 to 6 hours, until doubled in volume.

8. **PREPARE A LOAF PAN:** Line a loaf pan with parchment trimmed to fit (see step 6 of Zucchini Spice Quick Bread on page 44) or liberally grease the loaf pan.

9. **SHAPE:** Lightly flour a work surface. Divide the lighter colored dough in half. Using a rolling pin, roll one of the halves into a 10-by-12-inch rectangular shape. Divide the darker colored dough in half. Take one of the halves and roll out to the same size, then lay it on top of the rolled-out lighter dough. Repeat with the second half of each dough so that you have four layers with dark and light dough alternating. Take the short (10-inch) side of the dough and roll the dough into a cylinder. Press or pinch the seam to seal and place the dough seam-side down. Press the coiled ends down and seal them to the bottom of the loaf. Place the shaped dough in the prepared loaf pan.

10. **PROOF:** Cover and proof for 1½ to 3 hours, until the dough rises to the top of the loaf pan.

11. **PREHEAT:** About 20 to 30 minutes before the proofing is done, put a steam pan filled with water on the bottom oven rack and preheat the oven to 500°F.

12. **BAKE:** Place the loaf pan in the oven and quickly spray the oven walls with water. Reduce the oven temperature to 450°F and bake for 20 minutes. Remove the steam pan and bake for 15 to 20 minutes longer, until the loaf is a deep brown color. If the top is browning too quickly, tent aluminum foil over the top of the pan.

13. **COOL:** Place the loaf on a cooling rack and cool for at least 1 hour before slicing.

TIP: If you would like your bread to be done faster, you can add ¼ teaspoon or 2 grams of instant yeast when the starter is added. This will shorten the bulk ferment time to 1½ to 2 hours and the proof time to 45 to 75 minutes.

CHEESE-FILLED CHALLAH

Yield: 2 loaves

PREP TIME: 35 TO 45 MINUTES | **INACTIVE TIME:** 11 TO 16 HOURS | **BAKE TIME:** 35 TO 40 MINUTES

TOOLS NEEDED: food scale, food container, large bowl, spoon, plastic dough scraper, baking sheet, parchment paper, rolling pin, steam pan, small bowl, pastry brush, spray bottle, cooling rack

---

Shavuot is a time to celebrate tradition and remember the promise of the land of milk and honey. Some families enjoy challah that is baked with dairy, which is avoided during other feasts that mark the year. This challah is soft and full of beautiful rosemary flavor and melted, savory cheese.

FOR THE STARTER

30 grams sourdough starter (2 tablespoons) or ⅛ teaspoon instant yeast

15 grams white cane sugar (1 tablespoon)

50 grams water (3½ tablespoons)

100 grams all-purpose flour (⅔ cup)

FOR THE DOUGH

100 grams warm water, divided (about ½ cup)

3 grams instant yeast (1 teaspoon) (may be omitted—see Focaccia Picnic Sandwiches tips on page 55)

150 grams starter (about ¾ cup)

50 grams white cane sugar or honey (¼ cup)

500 grams bread flour (3½ cups)

70 grams oil, such as olive oil or avocado oil (⅓ cup)

3 large eggs

10 grams salt (1½ teaspoons)

6 grams fresh rosemary, minced (1 to 2 tablespoons)

FOR THE FILLING

200 grams mozzarella cheese, grated (2½ cups, loosely filled)

40 grams Parmesan cheese, freshly grated (⅔ cup, loosely filled)

FOR THE EGG WASH

1 large egg

⅛ teaspoon water

20 to 30 grams mozzarella cheese, grated, for topping (about ¼ cup)

1. **MAKE THE STARTER:** About 8 to 12 hours before mixing your dough, combine the starter or yeast, sugar, water, and flour in a clean container. Cover and leave at room temperature. It will increase in volume and become bubbly.

2. **WEIGH THE INGREDIENTS:** Making sure to tare after each addition, combine 90 grams of warm water, the instant yeast, 150 grams of starter, and the sugar. Allow the sugar to dissolve, then add the bread flour.

3. **MIX:** Mix the ingredients until a shaggy dough forms, then add the oil, the eggs, the salt, the remaining 10 grams of water, and the rosemary. Mix to combine.

4. **KNEAD:** Turn the dough out onto a work surface and knead by hand for 10 to 15 minutes or 3 to 8 minutes with a dough hook in a stand mixer, until the dough is smooth, is no longer sticky, and releases easily from the bowl or work surface.

5. **BULK FERMENT:** Cover the dough and ferment for 1½ to 2 hours, until doubled in volume.

6. **DIVIDE THE DOUGH:** Divide the dough into four equal pieces for two medium-size loaves.

7. **SHAPE:** Line a baking sheet with parchment paper. Lightly flour a work surface and roll out a piece of dough into a 9-by-7-inch rectangle. Sprinkle on one-quarter of the grated mozzarella and Parmesan cheeses, leaving at least 1-inch clear around the edges. Take the long edge of the rectangle and fold it up over the cheese. Pinch the edges together to seal around the cheese to make one length of dough. Repeat the filling and folding with another piece of dough. Take the two filled lengths of dough and intertwine them. Pinch the ends together to seal. Place on one side of the parchment-lined baking sheet. Repeat with the rest of the dough and cheese.

8. **PROOF:** Cover and proof for 45 to 60 minutes, until the bread is about 1½ times larger. Touching the dough with a fingertip should leave an indentation.

9. **PREHEAT:** Preheat the oven to 350°F. Place a steam pan filled with water on the lowest rack.

10. **MAKE THE EGG WASH:** Beat together the egg with the water and brush the mixture onto the challah. Then sprinkle the mozzarella on top.

11. **BAKE:** Place the loaves in the oven and quickly spray the oven walls with water. Bake for 25 minutes. Remove the steam pan and continue baking for 10 to 15 minutes longer, until the loaves are a shiny golden brown.

12. **COOL:** Transfer to a cooling rack and cool for 1 hour before serving.

BAVARIAN-INSPIRED PRETZEL ROLLS

Yield: 8 rolls

PREP TIME: 50 TO 60 MINUTES | **INACTIVE TIME:** 2 TO 3 HOURS | **BAKE TIME:** 15 TO 18 MINUTES

TOOLS NEEDED: food scale, large bowl, spoon, parchment paper, baking sheet, plastic dough scraper, wide pot, large slotted spoon, small bowl, pastry brush, bread lame or serrated bread knife, cooling rack

Bavarian-inspired pretzel rolls are quite nostalgic in our family, reminding us of trips we've taken. Now, when we make them at home, it signals to everyone that we are having a special meal, even if it's just another summer night together. They taste delicious with some butter or as a unique hot dog bun.

FOR THE DOUGH

330 grams warm water, divided (1½ cups plus 2 tablespoons)

15 grams honey (1 tablespoon)

4 grams instant yeast (1 teaspoon)

550 grams bread flour (3⅔ cups)

50 grams whole-wheat flour (⅓ cup)

42 grams unsalted butter, at room temperature (3 tablespoons)

10 grams salt (1½ teaspoons)

FOR POACHING

6 to 8 cups water

3 tablespoons baking soda

FOR THE EGG WASH

1 large egg

½ teaspoon water

1 to 3 teaspoons coarse salt, for topping

1. **WEIGH THE INGREDIENTS:** Making sure to tare your mixing bowl after each addition, combine 320 grams of warm water, the honey, instant yeast, bread flour, and whole-wheat flour in a mixing bowl.

2. **MIX:** Mix the ingredients until a shaggy dough forms, then add the butter, salt, and remaining 10 grams of water. Mix to combine.

3. **KNEAD:** Knead the dough for 10 to 15 minutes by hand or 3 to 8 minutes with a dough hook in an electric stand mixer, until the dough is smooth, is no longer sticky, and releases easily from the bowl or work surface.

4. **BULK FERMENT:** Cover the dough and ferment for 1½ to 2 hours, until it has doubled in volume.

5. **PREPARE THE BAKING SHEET:** Place a large piece of parchment paper on a flat baking sheet.

6. **SHAPE:** On an unfloured work surface, dividethe dough into 8 pieces (about 120 grams each). Shape the dough pieces into round balls. Flip a ball upside down and press down gently to flatten and form it into a rough square shape. Fold the top two corners into the middle at right angles to create a triangle shape. Fold the triangle top down, then fold the left and right sides of the dough to meet the triangle sides in the center. Fold the top edge of the dough to meet the bottom edge nearest you. Pinch the seam, then roll the dough back and forth to tighten and lengthen until it's about 5 to 6 inches long. Set the shaped dough, seam-side down, on the parchment paper–lined baking sheet. Repeat with the remaining balls of dough.

7. **PROOF:** Cover and proof for 30 to 60 minutes, until the dough is about 1½ times larger in volume. Touching the dough with a fingertip should leave an indentation.

8. **PREHEAT:** Preheat the oven to 400°F.

9. **POACH:** Bring the water to a boil in a large pot and add the baking soda. Add 1 or 2 of the proofed rolls. Boil for 30 seconds, then flip with a slotted spoon and boil for 30 more seconds. Put the poached rolls back on the parchment paper–lined baking sheet. Repeat with the remaining rolls.

10. **MAKE THE EGG WASH:** Beat the egg and water together and brush the mixture over the pretzel rolls.

11. **SCORE:** With a bread lame, slice 3 diagonal lines across the top of each roll of dough about ¼ inch deep. Top with the coarse salt.

12. **BAKE:** Place the rolls in the oven and bake for 15 to 18 minutes, until the outsides are a molasses brown color.

13. **COOL:** Place the rolls on a cooling rack and cool for 20 to 30 minutes before serving.

TIP: You can top these rolls with seeds instead of coarse salt, if desired.

ROSEMARY-TOMATO FOCACCIA

Yield: 1 large loaf

PREP TIME: 35 TO 40 MINUTES | **INACTIVE TIME:** 8½ TO 16 HOURS | **BAKE TIME:** 25 TO 30 MINUTES

TOOLS NEEDED: food scale, 2 large bowls, spoon, plastic dough scraper, parchment paper, steam pan, baking stone or sheet, bread peel, cooling rack

---

This bread is a delicious way to turn summer tomatoes and herbs into a lunch or dinner shared with friends. It is best enjoyed with fresh olive oil and a strong balsamic vinegar.

FOR THE STARTER
15 grams sourdough starter
(1 tablespoon) or ⅛ teaspoon
instant yeast

60 grams water (¼ cup
plus 3 tablespoons)

60 grams all-purpose
flour (⅔ cup)

FOR THE DOUGH
370 grams warm water, divided
(1½ cups plus 1 tablespoon)

15 grams white cane sugar
or honey (1 tablespoon)

2 grams instant yeast
(½ teaspoon)

100 grams starter (½ cup)

450 grams all-purpose flour
(3 cups plus 3½ tablespoons)

50 grams whole-wheat
flour (⅓ cup)

10 grams salt (1½ teaspoons)

40 grams olive oil, plus
more for the pan
(3½ tablespoons)

6 grams fresh rosemary,
minced (1 to 2 tablespoons)

FOR THE TOP
20 to 30 grams olive oil or
avocado oil (2 to 3 tablespoons)

200 to 250 grams grape
tomatoes, halved (½ to 1 cup)

10 to 15 grams coarse sea salt,
for topping (1 to 2 teaspoons)

1. **MAKE THE STARTER:** About 6 to 10 hours before mixing your dough, mix together the starter or yeast, water, and flour in a bowl. Cover and leave at room temperature until doubled in volume and bubbly.

2. **WEIGH THE INGREDIENTS:** Making sure to tare your bowl after each addition, combine 360 grams of warm water, the sugar, instant yeast, and 100 grams of starter. Let the sugar dissolve, then add the all-purpose flour and whole-wheat flour.

3. **MIX:** Stir the ingredients together until a shaggy dough forms, then add the salt, oil, and rosemary. Pour the remaining 10 grams of water over the salt to dissolve it. Mix to combine.

4. **FOLD:** Gather a portion of the dough, stretch it up, and fold it over the bulk. Rotate the bowl 90 degrees and repeat for 5 to 10 minutes or use a dough hook in a stand mixer for 4 to 8 minutes, until the dough

is smooth, is no longer sticky, and releases easily from the bowl.

5. **BULK FERMENT:** Place the dough in a clean bowl, cover, and ferment for 1½ to 2 hours, until doubled in volume.

6. **SHAPE:** Spread about 1 tablespoon of oil on a piece of parchment paper with your fingertips. Place the dough on the oiled parchment. Gently spread the dough with oiled fingertips into a 10-inch wide circle with uniform thickness. If the dough resists shaping, allow it to relax for 10 minutes. Top the bread with the oil, using your fingertips to make dimples in the dough. Evenly spread the tomatoes across the top of the bread, cut-side up, and gently press them down into the dough.

7. **PROOF:** Proof for 30 to 60 minutes at room temperature.

8. **PREHEAT:** After 30 minutes of proofing, preheat the oven to 475°F with a steam pan filled with water on a lower rack and a baking stone on the center rack (or you can bake your loaf on a baking sheet).

9. **BAKE:** Before the focaccia goes into the oven, sprinkle the top with the coarse salt. Use a bread peel or baking sheet to transfer the focaccia and parchment to the preheated baking stone. Close the oven and reduce the temperature to 450°F. Bake for 25 to 30 minutes, removing the steam pan after 10 minutes.

10. **COOL:** Allow the loaf to cool for 30 to 60 minutes on a cooling rack before serving.

TIP: Instant yeast can be omitted to create a naturally fermented bread if you are using sourdough starter. Timing will be 2 to 3 times longer for the fermentation and proofing processes.

Skillet Cinnamon-Apple Bread, page 95

Chapter Four

FALL

After the busy summer and start of school year, I look forward to what fall breads represent: spending time with family around the table and talking about the most important things.

SOUR CREAM BANANA BREAD WITH CANDIED PECANS

Yield: 1 loaf

PREP TIME: 25 TO 30 MINUTES | **INACTIVE TIME:** 10 TO 20 MINUTES | **BAKE TIME:** 55 TO 65 MINUTES

TOOLS NEEDED: food scale, knife, small pot, 2 small bowls, fork,
2 large mixing bowls, spoon, loaf pan, parchment paper, spatula

---

This is not just another banana bread recipe. When I share this bread with my family, it hardly makes it to the table before slices start disappearing. It has some traditional fall spices, but it can be enjoyed for any special occasion year-round.

FOR THE CANDIED PECANS

50 grams pecans (½ cup)

28 grams unsalted butter
(2 tablespoons)

30 grams white cane
sugar (2 tablespoons)

FOR THE DOUGH

2 large ripe bananas

4 grams vanilla
extract (1 teaspoon)

2 grams ground cinnamon
(½ teaspoon)

1 gram ground nutmeg
(¼ teaspoon)

150 grams all-purpose
flour (1 cup)

100 grams whole-wheat
flour (⅔ cup)

2 grams baking soda
(½ teaspoon)

2 grams salt (¼ teaspoon)

56 grams unsalted butter, at
room temperature (¼ cup)

100 grams brown sugar (½ cup)

50 grams white cane
sugar (¼ cup)

130 grams full-fat sour
cream (½ cup)

2 large eggs

1. **PREHEAT:** Preheat the oven to 375°F.

2. **MAKE THE CANDIED PECANS:** Roughly chop the pecans into ¼- to ½-inch pieces. Melt the 28 grams of butter over medium heat. Add the pecans and toss them in the butter to coat, then add the sugar. Continue to stir for 2 to 3 minutes, until the pecans are toasted and covered in sugar. Pour the candied pecans into a small bowl to cool. Set aside.

3. **MASH THE BANANAS:** Peel the bananas and place them in a small bowl. Mash with a fork. Add the vanilla extract, cinnamon, and nutmeg. Mash everything together until nearly smooth with a few lumps. Set aside.

4. **COMBINE THE DRY INGREDIENTS:** In a separate mixing bowl, stir together the all-purpose flour, whole-wheat flour, baking soda, and salt. Set aside.

5. **CREAM THE BUTTER AND SUGAR:** Put the 56 grams of butter in a mixing bowl or stand mixer and stir until smooth and creamy. Add the brown sugar and white sugar and mix until it is a smooth, creamy mixture. Stir in the sour cream and eggs.

6. **MIX:** Add the banana mixture to the butter mixture. Fold in. Slowly stir in the dry ingredients until well combined, being careful not to overmix.

7. **PREPARE THE LOAF PAN:** Line a loaf pan with parchment paper and set aside. (See step 6 of Zucchini Spice Quick Bread on page 44.)

8. **FILL THE LOAF PAN:** Use a spatula or spoon to add the batter to the loaf pan. Evenly distribute the candied pecans on top.

9. **BAKE:** Place the pan in the oven and bake for 55 to 65 minutes, until a toothpick or knife inserted into the center comes out clean.

10. **COOL:** Allow the loaf to cool for 10 to 20 minutes before slicing and serving.

TIPS: Rather than lining the loaf pan with parchment, you can generously grease the loaf pan with oil or butter.
To create a nut-free streusel topping, see step 10 of the Apple Fritter Quick Bread recipe (page 69).

APPLE FRITTER QUICK BREAD

Yield: 1 loaf

PREP TIME: 25 TO 35 MINUTES | **INACTIVE TIME:** 20 MINUTES | **BAKE TIME:** 70 TO 75 MINUTES

TOOLS NEEDED: 2 small bowls, food scale, 2 large mixing bowls,
spoon, loaf pan, parchment paper, spatula, whisk

*Apple fritters are usually a treat found only at the donut shop or
state fair, but this recipe will give you the same delicious flavors
at home. Apple fritter quick bread is great for sharing at breakfast,
for gifting to a friend, or even as an extra-special dessert.*

FOR THE APPLE-CINNAMON MIXTURE

1 Granny Smith or other green apple, peeled and diced into ¼- to ½-inch pieces (170 to 190 grams)

15 grams white cane sugar (1 tablespoon)

3 grams ground cinnamon (1 teaspoon)

FOR THE BATTER

300 grams all-purpose flour (2 cups)

50 grams brown sugar (¼ cup)

50 grams white cane sugar (¼ cup)

16 grams baking powder (1 tablespoon)

3 grams salt (½ teaspoon)

2 large eggs

170 grams whole milk (¾ cup)

2 grams vanilla extract (½ teaspoon)

84 grams unsalted butter, melted (6 tablespoons)

FOR THE STREUSEL

17 grams unsalted butter, melted (1½ tablespoons)

45 grams brown sugar (3 tablespoons)

FOR THE VANILLA GLAZE

65 grams powdered sugar (about ½ cup)

¼ teaspoon vanilla extract

1 to 3 teaspoons milk

1. **PREHEAT:** Preheat the oven to 350°F.
2. **PREPARE THE APPLE-CINNAMON MIXTURE:** In a small bowl, mix together the diced apple, sugar, and cinnamon until combined.
3. **WEIGH THE INGREDIENTS:** Making sure to tare after each addition, combine the flour, brown sugar, white sugar, baking powder, and salt in a large mixing bowl.
4. **STIR:** Stir the dry ingredients together and make a well in the center. Set aside.
5. **MIX THE WET INGREDIENTS:** In a second mixing bowl, mix together the eggs, milk, vanilla, and melted butter.
6. **ADD THE WET INGREDIENTS:** Pour the wet ingredient mixture into the well in the center of the dry mixture.
7. **STIR:** Stir everything together to make a thick batter, making sure all ingredients are well dispersed throughout. Don't overmix.

8. **PREPARE THE LOAF PAN:** Line a loaf pan with parchment paper and set aside. (See step 6 of Zucchini Spice Quick Bread on page 44.)

9. **FILL THE LOAF PAN:** Using a spatula, add half of the batter to the loaf pan, spreading to evenly fill the bottom of the pan. Top with half of the apple-cinnamon mixture, gently pressing the apples down into the batter. Add the rest of the batter, spreading to cover the apple layer. Then top with the rest of the apple-cinnamon mixture.

10. **MAKE THE STREUSEL:** Combine the melted butter and brown sugar in the small bowl that held the apple mixture. Stir with a fork, then evenly top the batter with the streusel.

11. **BAKE:** Place the pan in the oven and bake for 70 to 75 minutes. The bread should have a caramelized crust and golden-brown edges, and a toothpick or knife inserted into the center should come out clean.

12. **COOL:** Let the bread cool for about 20 minutes.

13. **PREPARE THE GLAZE:** While the bread is cooling, whisk the powdered sugar, vanilla, and milk together until it reaches a good consistency for drizzling. Drizzle generously over the cooled bread, then serve.

TIP: The parchment paper in the loaf pans makes the Apple Fritter Quick Bread easy to remove. Tie a ribbon around the loaf with a gift tag to give to a friend or neighbor.

PUMPKIN SPICE WAFFLES

Yield: 12 waffles

PREP TIME: 25 MINUTES | **BAKE TIME:** 2 TO 3 MINUTES PER WAFFLE

TOOLS NEEDED: 3 mixing bowls, food scale, spoon, electric whisk, waffle maker

Nearly every weekend in fall, I make this special version of our favorite breakfast. Make sure your spices are fresh to create the best flavors; for even more flavor, I love using freshly grated nutmeg.

4 large eggs

85 grams unsalted butter, melted (6 tablespoons)

336 grams pumpkin puree (1 cup)

30 grams honey (2 tablespoons)

60 grams brown sugar (¼ cup plus 2 teaspoons)

620 grams whole milk (2⅔ cups)

400 grams all-purpose flour (2¾ cups plus 1 tablespoon)

160 grams whole-wheat flour (1 cup plus 2 tablespoons)

8 grams salt (1¼ teaspoons)

12 grams baking powder (2 teaspoons)

9 grams ground cinnamon (1 tablespoon)

10 grams ground ginger (1 tablespoon plus 1 teaspoon)

2 grams ground nutmeg (1 teaspoon)

1 gram ground cloves (½ teaspoon)

1. **SEPARATE THE EGGS:** Crack the eggs and separate the whites and yolks into separate mixing bowls.

2. **PREHEAT THE WAFFLE MAKER ACCORDING TO MANUFACTURER'S INSTRUCTIONS.**

3. **WEIGH THE INGREDIENTS:** Tare the mixing bowl with the egg yolks. Combine the pumpkin puree, honey, brown sugar, and milk and stir well. Set aside.

4. **MIX THE DRY INGREDIENTS:** Tare another mixing bowl. Combine the all-purpose flour, whole-wheat flour, salt, baking powder, cinnamon, ginger, nutmeg, and cloves. Stir well.

5. **ADD THE WET INGREDIENTS:** Add the pumpkin mixture to the dry ingredients. Mix until well combined, but don't overmix. Set aside.

6. **BEAT THE EGG WHITES:** Use an electric whisk to beat the egg whites until they have soft peaks. Gently fold the whipped egg whites into the batter.

7. **COOK THE WAFFLES:** Scoop ⅓ to ½ cup of the batter onto the waffle iron, gently spread it, and close the lid. Cook according to your waffle maker manufacturer's instructions, usually 2 to 3 minutes.

8. **SERVE.**

EAST AFRICAN–INSPIRED CHAPATI FLATBREAD

Yield: 15 chapatis

PREP TIME: 35 TO 50 MINUTES | **INACTIVE TIME:** 25 TO 35 MINUTES
BAKE TIME: 1 TO 2 MINUTES PER CHAPATI

TOOLS NEEDED: food scale, large bowl, spoon, plastic dough scraper, rolling pin, small pot, pastry brush, large skillet or pan, serving plate

East African–inspired chapati flatbread are deliciously buttery and flakey. This is an easy recipe and is also a great bread to make for celebrating Diwali.

FOR THE DOUGH
275 grams warm water
(1 cup plus 3 tablespoons)
500 grams all-purpose
flour (3 cups)

80 grams ghee, melted
butter, or oil (⅓ cup)
10 grams salt
(1½ teaspoons)

FOR BRUSHING CHAPATI
4 to 5 tablespoons ghee
or melted butter

1. **WEIGH THE INGREDIENTS:** Tare a large bowl, and combine the warm water, flour, ghee, and salt.
2. **KNEAD:** Mix and knead the dough for 10 to 15 minutes (3 to 7 minutes in a stand mixer), until the dough is smooth.
3. **DIVIDE:** Divide the dough into 15 equal pieces (57 grams each). Roll each piece into a ball.
4. **REST:** Cover and let rest for 15 to 20 minutes.
5. **PRE-SHAPE:** Melt 4 to 5 tablespoons of ghee and set aside. Lightly flour the work surface and the rolling pin. Roll out a ball of dough into a very thin 8½- to 9-inch circle. Brush a thin layer of ghee onto the dough. Lightly dust with flour, then roll up tightly to make a long, thin tube. Coil the tube of dough into a tight spiral. Set aside. Repeat with the remaining balls of dough.
6. **REST:** Cover the dough and let rest for 10 to 15 minutes.
7. **HEAT THE SKILLET:** Heat a large pan or skillet over medium-high heat.
8. **FINAL SHAPE:** Roll out a piece of spiral dough with a rolling pin lightly dusted with flour. Chapati should be slightly thicker than a tortilla and about 7 inches wide.
9. **COOK:** Place a chapati on the hot skillet and cook for 30 seconds or until the bottom is cooked with brown spots. Flip and brush the cooked side with ghee. Once the other side is cooked, move the chapati to a serving plate and brush with ghee. Repeat steps 8 and 9 with the remaining pieces of dough.

NAVAJO-INSPIRED FRYBREAD

Yield: 16 frybreads

PREP TIME: 20 TO 30 MINUTES | **INACTIVE TIME:** 15 TO 20 MINUTES
BAKE TIME: 3 TO 4 MINUTES PER FRYBREAD

TOOLS NEEDED: food scale, mixing bowl, spoon, plastic dough scraper, rolling pin, candy thermometer or digital thermometer, medium pot, cooling rack, paper towels, large slotted metal spoon or spatula, timer, fork

This crispy treat can be made savory if used as a taco shell, or it can transform into a decadent dessert by adding honey, jam, cinnamon sugar, or powdered sugar. Making and enjoying this bread is a great way to honor Native American Heritage Month in November.

FOR THE DOUGH
320 grams warm water (1⅓ cups)
600 grams all-purpose flour (4 cups)

15 grams baking powder (1 tablespoon)
12 grams salt (2 teaspoons)

FOR FRYING
3 to 4 cups oil (e.g., vegetable, coconut, tallow)

1. **WEIGH THE INGREDIENTS:** Making sure to tare after each addition, combine the warm water, flour, baking powder, and salt in a mixing bowl.
2. **KNEAD:** Mix the dough well. Turn the dough out onto a work surface and knead for 8 to 12 minutes by hand or 4 to 6 minutes with a dough hook in a stand mixer, until the dough is smooth, is no longer sticky, and releases easily from the bowl or work surface.
3. **DIVIDE:** Divide the dough into 16 equal pieces. Roll each piece into a ball.
4. **REST:** Cover the dough and let it rest for 15 to 20 minutes.

5. **HEAT THE OIL:** Attach a thermometer to the side of a medium pot with at least a 2.75-quart capacity. Add the oil until the depth is at least 3 inches. Place the pot on the stovetop and heat the oil to 360°F.
6. **PREPARE A COOLING RACK:** While the oil is coming to temperature, line a cooling rack with paper towels and have a large slotted spoon and timer ready.
7. **SHAPE:** Take a ball of dough and roll it into a circle about 5 inches wide and about ¼ inch thick. Pierce the top of the rolled dough 3 or 4 times with a fork.

8. **FRY:** Add the disc of dough to the hot oil and cook for 1½ to 2 minutes, until the bottom side is golden brown and puffed up. Use a metal slotted spoon to turn the frybread over and fry on the other side for 1½ to 2 minutes, until browned. Remove the frybread from the oil with a slotted spoon and place it on the lined cooling rack.

9. **REPEAT:** Repeat steps 7 and 8 until all the frybread rounds have been fried.

TIP: For successful frying, monitor the temperature. If the temperature is too high, your frybread will be dense, underbaked in the center, and overdone on the outside. A frying temperature that is too low will result in an oily textured frybread.

ROTI FLATBREAD

Yield: 24 roti

PREP TIME: 35 TO 50 MINUTES | **INACTIVE TIME:** 15 TO 20 MINUTES
BAKE TIME: 2 TO 3 MINUTES PER ROTI

TOOLS NEEDED: food scale, large bowl, spoon, plastic dough scraper, rolling pin, large skillet or pan, fork or spatula, pastry brush, serving plate

Roti is a very popular flatbread in India and is often an important bread for serving with vegetarian and meat entrées. Full of flavor and with nutritious whole wheat, roti is an essential part of Diwali, as well as other annual festivals for many Indian families.

FOR THE DOUGH
260 grams very warm water
(1 cup plus 2 tablespoons)

400 grams whole-wheat
flour (2⅔ cups)

20 grams ghee, melted
butter, or oil (4 teaspoons)

8 grams salt
(1¼ teaspoons)

FOR BRUSHING ROTI
4 to 5 tablespoons ghee
or melted butter

1. **WEIGH THE INGREDIENTS:** Tare a mixing bowl; add the warm water, flour, ghee, and salt.

2. **KNEAD:** Mix the dough well. Turn the dough out onto a work surface and knead for 10 to 15 minutes by hand (3 to 6 minutes in a stand mixer) until the dough is smooth and releases easily from the bowl or work surface. To further soften the dough, hit it with a rolling pin 5 to 10 times.

3. **DIVIDE:** Divide the dough into 24 equal pieces. Roll each piece into a ball.

4. **REST:** Cover the dough and let it rest for 15 to 20 minutes.

5. **HEAT THE SKILLET:** Heat a large pan or skillet over medium-high heat.

6. **FINAL SHAPE:** Flour the work surface and a rolling pin. Roll out a piece of dough until very thin, about 6 to 6½ inches wide.

7. **COOK:** Place a dough round in the hot skillet and cook until bubbles form. Flip and cook for 20 to 30 seconds, until more bubbles form. Flip the roti back over and use a fork or spatula to press around the edges to make it begin to puff up. Brush the top with a light layer of ghee or butter, then flip over and repeat this process to allow it to puff up more. The goal is to have the roti completely puffed up. Place the cooked roti on a serving plate and cover with a cloth. Repeat with the remaining pieces of dough.

TIP: When mixing your dough, it is important to feel for the right texture and consistency. Knead the dough for 5 to 10 minutes before adjusting if it feels too wet. Usually, whole-wheat flour takes time to absorb liquid. If it feels too dry, add 1 teaspoon of water at a time and knead for 1 to 3 more minutes.

CONE-SHAPED ROLLS

Yield: 8 shaped rolls

PREP TIME: 45 TO 50 MINUTES | **INACTIVE TIME:** 13 TO 20 HOURS | **BAKE TIME:** 25 TO 30 MINUTES

TOOLS NEEDED: food scale, 2 large bowls, spoon, small pot, plastic dough scraper, 2 baking sheets, parchment paper, aluminum foil, small bowl, pastry brush, cooling rack

---

A special touch for Thanksgiving dinners is serving these cone-shaped rolls at each place setting. They can be filled with vegetables, a spinach dip, salad, or slices of roast turkey for a kid-friendly meal that everyone will love.

FOR THE STARTER
15 grams sourdough starter (1 tablespoon) or ⅛ teaspoon instant yeast
110 grams water (½ cup)
110 grams all-purpose flour (¾ cup)

FOR THE DOUGH
80 grams milk (⅓ cup)

110 grams warm water, divided (7½ tablespoons)
200 grams starter (about 1 cup)
5 grams white cane sugar (1 teaspoon)
4 grams instant yeast (1 teaspoon)
28 grams unsalted butter, at room temperature (2 tablespoons)

340 grams all-purpose flour (2¼ cups)
40 grams whole-wheat flour (⅓ cup)
8 grams salt (1¼ teaspoons)

FOR THE EGG WASH
1 large egg
¼ teaspoon water

1. **MAKE THE STARTER:** About 8 to 12 hours before mixing your dough, combine the starter or yeast, water, and flour in a bowl. Mix well, cover, and leave at room temperature in a warm place to allow the yeast to activate. It will become bubbly and double in volume.
2. **WARM THE MILK:** Heat the milk until it reaches a temperature of 110°F to 120°F.
3. **WEIGH THE INGREDIENTS:** Making sure to tare after each addition, combine 70 grams of warm milk, 100 grams of warm water, 200 grams of starter, the sugar, and the instant yeast in a mixing bowl.

Add the butter, all-purpose flour, and whole-wheat flour.
4. **MIX:** Mix the ingredients together until a shaggy dough forms, then add the salt and the remaining 10 grams of water. Mix to combine.
5. **KNEAD:** Turn the dough out onto a work surface and knead for 10 to 15 minutes by hand or 3 to 7 minutes with a dough hook in a stand mixer, until the dough is smooth, is no longer sticky, and releases easily from the bowl or work surface.

CONTINUED ON NEXT PAGE

6. **BULK FERMENT:** Cover the dough and leave it to ferment for 1½ to 2 hours, until it has doubled in volume.

7. **PREPARE THE BAKING SHEETS:** Line two flat baking sheets with parchment paper and set aside.

8. **PREPARE THE MOLDS:** Cut 8 squares of aluminum foil. Crumple and fold each foil sheet into a cone shape about 4½ inches tall with a top that is about 2 to 2½ inches across.

9. **DIVIDE:** Divide the dough into 8 equal pieces (about 98 grams each).

10. **SHAPE:** Transfer the dough to a work surface. Roll a piece of dough under your hands until it becomes a 25-inch rope. Start at the top of the foil cone and wrap the dough around the outside. Pinch the first coil to seal the loop, then wrap the dough around the cone, keeping the coiled layers tight together. Once you get to the bottom, pinch the ends to close the tip of the cone shape. (If you run out of dough, you can gently push the coiled layers down the cone closer to the tip.) Place the wrapped cone on its side on one of the parchment paper–lined baking sheets. Repeat with the remaining pieces of dough. There should be 4 shaped rolls on each baking sheet, spaced at least 3 inches apart.

11. **PROOF:** Cover and proof in a warm place for 45 to 60 minutes, until the layers of the rolls are puffy.

12. **PREHEAT:** Preheat the oven to 375°F. If your oven can't fit both sheets, put one in the refrigerator while the other is baking.

13. **MAKE THE EGG WASH:** In a small bowl, beat the egg and water together until combined. Brush over the dough, getting between the layers but avoiding getting any egg wash on the foil.

14. **BAKE:** Place one of the baking sheets in the preheated oven. Bake for 20 to 25 minutes or until golden brown. Remove to a cooling rack and swap in the other sheet of rolls.

15. **COOL:** Cool for 10 to 15 minutes, then carefully remove the foil cones.

16. **SECOND BAKE:** Bake for 5 more minutes without the foil. This will increase the cones' durability when you're filling them.

SWEET POTATO BUNS

Yield: 16 rolls

PREP TIME: 60 TO 75 MINUTES | **INACTIVE TIME:** 2½ TO 3½ HOURS | **BAKE TIME:** 16 TO 18 MINUTES

TOOLS NEEDED: 2 baking sheets, parchment paper, knife, food scale, large bowl, spoon, small pot, plastic dough scraper, small bowl, pastry brush, spray bottle

---

Sweet potato, brown sugar, and nutmeg are a beautiful fall flavor combination. These sweet potato buns would be great with any fall feast or as festive slider buns for Halloween. We enjoy them topped with shredded barbecue chicken, a strong cheese, and cilantro.

FOR THE SWEET POTATO MASH

1 large sweet potato (such as garnet yam) or 2 small sweet potatoes

1 to 2 teaspoons ghee or oil

FOR THE DOUGH

280 grams mashed sweet potato (about 1 cup, after mashing)

120 grams milk (¼ cup plus 3 tablespoons)

100 grams warm water, divided (¼ cup plus 3 tablespoons)

50 grams brown sugar (¼ cup)

8 grams instant yeast (2 teaspoons)

450 grams all-purpose flour (3 cups)

90 grams whole-wheat flour (⅔ cup)

2 grams ground nutmeg (½ teaspoon)

57 grams unsalted butter, at room temperature (4 tablespoons)

10 grams salt (1½ teaspoons)

2 large eggs

FOR THE EGG WASH

1 large egg

⅛ teaspoon water

Pinch salt

---

1. **COOK THE SWEET POTATOES:** Preheat the oven to 425°F. Line a baking sheet with parchment paper. Cut a large sweet potato (or two small sweet potatoes) in half the long way. Lightly grease the parchment with ghee or oil, then place the potatoes cut-side down on the baking sheet. Bake for 25 to 30 minutes or until fork-tender. Allow to cool before mashing.

2. **WEIGH THE POTATOES:** Once the roasted sweet potatoes are cool enough to handle, tare a mixing bowl and scoop 280 grams of sweet potato into the bowl.

3. **MASH THE POTATOES:** Mash the potatoes until very smooth, either by hand or using a stand mixer.

4. **WARM THE MILK:** Heat the milk until it reaches a temperature of 115°F to 120°F.

5. **WEIGH THE INGREDIENTS:** Making sure to tare after each addition, add 100 grams of warm milk, 90 grams of warm water, the brown sugar, and the instant yeast to the mashed sweet potatoes. Allow the sugar to

CONTINUED ON NEXT PAGE

dissolve. Finally, add the all-purpose flour, whole-wheat flour, and nutmeg.

6. **MIX:** Mix the ingredients together until a shaggy dough forms, then add the butter, salt, remaining 10 grams of water, and eggs. Mix to combine.

7. **FOLD:** Stretch sections of the dough and fold over repeatedly to develop the gluten, until the dough no longer sticks to the sides of the bowl and pulls away easily. Do this by hand for 5 to 10 minutes or 3 to 6 minutes with a dough hook in a stand mixer.

8. **BULK FERMENT:** Cover the dough and ferment for 1½ to 2 hours, until doubled in volume.

9. **PREPARE THE BAKING SHEETS:** Line two baking sheets with parchment paper and set aside.

10. **DIVIDE:** On a floured work surface, divide the dough into 16 equal pieces (about 70 grams each).

11. **SHAPE:** Gently flatten a piece of the dough with your hand, then gather the edges into the center and pinch together to seal. Turn the dough over onto the seam and rotate under your hand, using gentle but quick circular rotations, until the dough is a smooth ball. Place it on one of the parchment paper–lined baking sheets. Repeat with the remaining pieces of dough, placing them 3 to 4 inches apart.

12. **PROOF:** Cover the shaped rolls and proof for 30 to 60 minutes, until puffy and at least 1½ times larger.

13. **PREHEAT:** Preheat the oven to 375°F.

14. **MAKE THE EGG WASH:** Beat together the egg, water, and salt in a small bowl or cup. Using a pastry brush, brush the egg wash all over the tops of the rolls.

15. **BAKE:** Place the rolls in the preheated oven, spray the walls of the oven with water, and close the oven door. Bake for 16 to 18 minutes, until the rolls are golden brown on top.

16. **COOL:** Let the rolls cool for at least 15 minutes.

TIP: These rolls can be frozen to prepare in advance. Follow the recipe through step 12. Once the rolls are done proofing, place the covered baking sheets in the freezer. If freezing for longer than a day, wait for the rolls to set, then move them to a freezer bag to store for up to 3 months. To bake, preheat the oven as directed in step 13 and bake the rolls straight from the freezer for 20 minutes. The egg wash step will be omitted.

PARKER HOUSE ROLLS

Yield: 16 rolls

PREP TIME: 45 TO 50 MINUTES | **INACTIVE TIME:** 13 TO 20 HOURS | **BAKE TIME:** 12 TO 14 MINUTES

TOOLS NEEDED: food scale, 2 large bowls, small pot, spoon, plastic dough scraper, 2 baking sheets, parchment paper, rolling pin, small bowl, pastry brush

---

Parker House rolls are buttery rolls that originated in a once-famous hotel in Boston. They are known for their soft, fluffy texture and rich, buttery flavor. They are made to be part of a Thanksgiving dinner. See the tips at the end of the recipe for some ways to make these ahead of time when prepping for a big holiday meal.

FOR THE STARTER
15 grams sourdough starter (1 tablespoon) or
⅛ teaspoon instant yeast
110 grams water (½ cup)
110 grams all-purpose flour (¾ cup)

FOR THE DOUGH
190 grams milk (¾ cup)

20 grams white cane sugar (1 tablespoon plus 1 teaspoon)
3 grams instant yeast (1 teaspoon)
200 grams starter (about 1 cup)
400 grams all-purpose flour (2⅔ cups)
1 large egg yolk

8 grams salt (1¼ teaspoons)
110 grams unsalted butter, at room temperature, divided (8 tablespoons)

FOR THE TOPPING
56 grams unsalted butter (4 tablespoons)
15 grams honey (1 tablespoon)

1. **MAKE THE STARTER:** About 8 to 12 hours before mixing your dough, combine the starter or yeast, water, and flour in a bowl. Mix well, cover, and leave at room temperature in a warm place to allow the yeast to activate. It will become bubbly and double in volume.

2. **WARM THE MILK:** Heat the milk until it reaches a temperature of 110°F to 120°F.

3. **WEIGH THE INGREDIENTS:** Making sure to tare after each addition, combine 170 grams of warm milk, the sugar, the instant yeast, and 200 grams of starter in a mixing bowl. Once the sugar is dissolved, add the flour.

4. **MIX:** Mix the ingredients together until a shaggy dough is formed, then add the egg yolk and salt. Mix to combine.

5. **ADD THE BUTTER:** Fold in 56 grams of butter.

6. **KNEAD:** Turn the dough out onto a work surface and knead for 10 to 15 minutes by hand or 3 to 7 minutes with a dough hook in a stand mixer, until the dough is smooth, is no longer sticky, and releases easily from the bowl or work surface.

7. **BULK FERMENT:** Cover the dough and ferment for 1½ to 2 hours, until doubled in volume.

CONTINUED ON NEXT PAGE

8. **PREPARE THE BAKING SHEETS:** Line two large baking sheets with parchment paper.

9. **DIVIDE:** Divide the dough into 16 pieces (about 54 grams each). Roll each into a ball.

10. **SHAPE:** With a rolling pin, roll a piece of dough into a 3-inch circle. Add a thinly cut piece (about 4 grams) of butter to the center of the circle, then fold over until the edge is just ¼ inch short of meeting the other edge. Press the fold down to seal. Place the shaped roll on one of the prepared baking sheets. Repeat this step with the remaining pieces of dough.

11. **PROOF:** Cover and proof in a warm place for 45 to 60 minutes, until the rolls appear puffy and an indentation is left on the dough when pressed.

12. **PREHEAT:** Preheat the oven to 425°F.

13. **BAKE:** Place the rolls in the preheated oven. Bake for 12 to 14 minutes, until golden brown.

14. **MAKE THE HONEY BUTTER TOPPING:** While the rolls are baking, melt the butter for the topping. Add the honey and stir. Brush it onto the rolls right when you take them out of the oven.

15. **COOL:** Allow the rolls to cool and soak in the butter for 5 to 10 minutes before serving.

TIPS: Instant yeast can be omitted to create a naturally fermented bread. The fermentation and proofing times will be 2 to 3 times longer if using this method.
To make this dough ahead of time, cover and refrigerate for up to 2 days after kneading. Shaped rolls can be refrigerated for 4 to 6 hours or overnight to proof and can be baked without coming to room temperature. Shaped rolls can be frozen and baked straight from the freezer with a baking time of 14 to 18 minutes.

PAN DULCE CONCHAS
(SWEET SHELL BREAD)

Yield: 10 large rolls

PREP TIME: 50 TO 65 MINUTES | **INACTIVE TIME:** 3 TO 4 HOURS | **BAKE TIME:** 20 TO 22 MINUTES

TOOLS NEEDED: saucepan or small pot, food scale, large bowl, spoon, plastic dough scraper, 2 baking sheets, parchment paper, concha press or knife, cooling rack

These traditional pan dulce conchas are delicious and fun to make. My kids love cutting patterns into the tops and picking their favorite flavors (mine is cinnamon). Enjoy these with family and friends for Día de los Muertos or another festive occasion.

FOR THE DOUGH

210 grams milk, divided (¾ cup plus 2 tablespoons)

100 grams white cane sugar (½ cup)

4 grams instant yeast (1 teaspoon)

550 grams all-purpose flour (3⅔ cups)

24 grams lard, at room temperature (2 tablespoons)

85 grams unsalted butter, at room temperature (6 tablespoons)

4 grams vanilla extract (1 teaspoon)

6 grams salt (1 teaspoon)

2 large eggs

FOR THE TOPPING

75 grams powdered sugar (½ cup)

75 grams all-purpose flour (½ cup)

1 gram baking powder (¼ teaspoon)

45 grams lard, at room temperature (3 tablespoons)

24 grams unsalted butter, at room temperature, plus extra to brush on rolls (2 tablespoons)

2 grams vanilla extract (⅓ teaspoon)

1 to 2 grams ground cinnamon or cocoa powder (¼ to ½ teaspoon) (optional)

Food coloring (optional)

1. **WARM THE MILK:** Heat the milk until it reaches a temperature of 115°F to 120°F.

2. **WEIGH THE INGREDIENTS:** Making sure to tare after each addition, combine 190 grams of warm milk, the sugar, and the instant yeast in a mixing bowl and allow the sugar to dissolve. Add the flour, lard, and butter.

3. **MIX:** Mix the ingredients together until a shaggy dough forms, then add the vanilla, salt, 10 grams of warm milk, and the eggs.

Discard any remaining milk. Mix until combined.

4. **KNEAD:** Turn the dough out onto a work surface and knead for 10 to 15 minutes by hand or 3 to 7 minutes with a dough hook in a stand mixer, until the dough is smooth, is no longer sticky, and releases easily from the bowl or work surface.

CONTINUED ON NEXT PAGE

5. **BULK FERMENT:** Cover the dough and ferment for 2 to 3½ hours, until doubled in volume. This dough is very rich, so give it time to rise.

6. **PREPARE THE BAKING SHEETS:** Line two flat baking sheets with parchment paper and set aside.

7. **MAKE THE TOPPING:** Making sure to tare after each addition, combine the powdered sugar, flour, and baking powder in a mixing bowl. Stir. Add the lard, butter, and vanilla. Mix until a very smooth paste is formed. To make different colors or flavors, divide the paste. If dividing in half for two flavors, add 2 grams of cinnamon or cocoa powder and mix. If dividing into thirds for three flavors, add 1 gram of cinnamon or cocoa powder. Food coloring can be added to the white vanilla paste dough, as well. Set aside until step 10.

8. **DIVIDE:** Divide the fermented pan dulce dough into 10 equal pieces (about 100 grams each).

9. **SHAPE:** Gently press each piece into a small disc, then fold the edges into the center, pinching together to form a seam. Turn the dough over onto the seam and rotate it with light pressure and quick movements until it becomes a smooth ball. Place the ball on one of the prepared baking sheets. Gently press down so that the roll is wider and stands about 1 inch high. Repeat with the remaining pieces of dough. Space the rolls 2 to 3 inches apart on the baking sheets.

10. **TOP:** Lightly grease the top of the rolls with butter. Divide the topping paste into 10 pieces weighing 20 grams each. Roll each piece into a ball, then pass back and forth between your palms, flattening into a thin disc wide enough to cover the tops of the rolls. Press the discs on top of each of the rolls. Cut a pattern into the paste with a concha press or use a regular table knife to cut curved lines or a crosshatch pattern into the topping paste. Avoid cutting the pan dulce dough.

11. **PROOF:** Cover the rolls with plastic wrap and proof in a warm place for 1 to 1½ hours, until at least 1½ times larger.

12. **PREHEAT:** Preheat the oven to 375°F.

13. **BAKE:** Place the rolls in the oven. Reduce the oven temperature to 350°F and bake for 20 to 22 minutes, until golden brown around the bottom edge.

14. **COOL:** Place the rolls on a cooling rack to cool for at least 20 minutes before serving.

TIP: Lard is a traditional ingredient, but if it's unavailable, unsalted butter or vegetable shortening can be substituted.

KANELBULLAR

Yield : 16 kanelbullar

PREP TIME: 50 TO 65 MINUTES | **INACTIVE TIME:** 11 TO 18 HOURS
BAKE TIME: 7 TO 10 MINUTES PER BATCH

TOOLS NEEDED: food scale, large bowl, spoon, plastic dough scraper, 2 baking sheets, parchment paper, 2 small bowls, rolling pin, rolling pizza cutter or knife, pastry brush, cooling rack

---

On October 4, Sweden celebrates Kanelbullar Day with festive cinnamon buns (also known as cinnamon snails). This type of sweet treat is enjoyed with coffee as part of what is called fika, *or sharing pastries and coffee while socializing. These delicious kanelbullar will have your friends and family lingering over the table.*

FOR THE STARTER
15 grams sourdough starter
(1 tablespoon) or
⅛ teaspoon instant yeast

60 grams water (¼ cup
plus 3 tablespoons)

60 grams all-purpose
flour (⅔ cup)

FOR THE DOUGH
230 grams milk (¾ cup
plus 2½ tablespoons)

100 grams starter
(about ½ cup)

70 grams white cane
sugar (⅓ cup)

4 grams instant yeast
(1 teaspoon)

500 grams
all-purpose flour (3½ cups)

4 grams ground cardamom
(1 teaspoon)

70 grams unsalted butter,
melted (5 tablespoons)

6 grams salt (1 teaspoon)

FOR THE FILLING
60 grams unsalted butter,
at room temperature
(4½ tablespoons)

100 grams white cane
sugar (½ cup)

8 grams ground cinnamon
(2 teaspoons)

FOR THE EGG WASH
1 large egg

⅛ teaspoon water

2 tablespoons pearl sugar or
sliced almonds (optional)

1. **MAKE THE STARTER:** About 6 to 12 hours before mixing your dough, combine the starter or yeast, water, and flour in a clean container. Cover and leave at room temperature. Once active, it will double in volume and become full of large bubbles.

2. **WARM THE MILK:** Heat the milk until it reaches a temperature of 110°F to 120°F.

3. **WEIGH THE INGREDIENTS:** Making sure to tare after each addition, combine 200 grams of warm milk, 100 grams of starter, the sugar, and the instant yeast in a mixing bowl. Allow the sugar to dissolve, then add the flour and cardamom.

CONTINUED ON NEXT PAGE

4. **MIX:** Mix the ingredients together until a shaggy dough forms, then add the melted butter and salt. Mix to combine.

5. **KNEAD:** Turn the dough out onto a work surface and knead for 10 to 15 minutes by hand or 4 to 8 minutes with a dough hook in a stand mixer, until the dough is smooth, is no longer sticky, and releases easily from the bowl or work surface.

6. **BULK FERMENT:** Cover the dough and ferment for 3 to 4 hours, until doubled in volume.

7. **PREPARE THE BAKING SHEETS:** Line two flat baking sheets with parchment paper and set aside.

8. **PREPARE THE FILLING:** Mix the butter, sugar, and cinnamon together until smooth. Set aside.

9. **SHAPE:** Place the dough on a lightly floured work surface. Dust flour onto a rolling pin and roll the dough into a 24-by-12-inch rectangle. Use a spatula to spread the filling evenly across the surface of the dough, leaving a ½-inch margin along the long sides. Fold the dough in half from the long edge and press to seal. With a rolling pizza cutter or knife, cut the dough from folded edge to sealed edge into 16 (1½-inch) strips. Gently stretch a dough piece out and twist tightly about 8 times, then twist one end around the other. Press the edges of the strip underneath to seal. Place the knot on one of the prepared baking sheets. Repeat with the remaining strips of dough.

10. **PROOF:** Cover and proof for 1½ to 2½ hours, until about 1½ times larger in volume. Touching the dough should leave an indentation when it is finished proofing.

11. **PREHEAT:** Preheat the oven to 425°F.

12. **MAKE THE EGG WASH:** Beat the egg and water together. Brush all over the kanelbullar knots to cover every crevice. Sprinkle with pearl sugar or sliced almonds (if using).

13. **BAKE:** Place the first baking sheet in the oven and bake for 7 to 10 minutes, until the knots are golden brown. Move the cooked kanelbullar to a cooling rack and move the second sheet of kanelbullar to the oven to bake.

14. **COOL AND SERVE:** Allow the kanelbullar to cool for about 10 minutes. Serve fresh with coffee.

TIP: Instant yeast can be omitted to create a naturally fermented bread. The fermentation and proofing process will take about 2 times longer with this method.

EVERYTHING BAGELS

Yield: 8 bagels

PREP TIME: 35 TO 50 MINUTES | **INACTIVE TIME:** 2 TO 3 HOURS | **BAKE TIME:** 15 TO 20 MINUTES

TOOLS NEEDED: food scale, large bowl, spoon, plastic dough scraper, 2 baking sheets, parchment paper, large pot, large slotted spoon or spatula, small bowl, pastry brush, cooling rack

Yom Kippur is a sacred day of fasting and reflection, which is followed by celebration. Everything bagels are easy to put together for a special breakfast following Yom Kippur. Enjoy with butter, cream cheese, eggs, or some smoked salmon.

FOR THE DOUGH
270 grams warm water, divided (1 cup plus 2 tablespoons plus 1 teaspoon)

12 grams instant yeast (1½ teaspoons)

30 grams brown sugar (2 tablespoons)

50 grams whole-wheat flour (⅓ cup)

450 grams bread flour (3 cups)

12 grams salt (2 teaspoons)

FOR POACHING THE BAGELS
1 tablespoon baking soda

FOR THE EGG WASH
1 egg

¼ teaspoon water

2 to 3 tablespoons everything bagel seasoning

1. **WEIGH THE INGREDIENTS:** Making sure to tare after each addition, combine 260 grams of warm water, the instant yeast, brown sugar, whole-wheat flour, and bread flour in a mixing bowl.

2. **MIX:** Mix the ingredients together until a shaggy dough forms, then add the salt and the remaining 10 grams of water. Mix to combine.

3. **KNEAD:** Turn the dough out onto a work surface and knead for 10 to 15 minutes by hand or 4 to 8 minutes with a dough hook in a stand mixer, until the dough is smooth, is no longer sticky, and releases easily from the bowl or work surface.

4. **BULK FERMENT:** Cover the dough and leave it in a warm place to ferment for 1½ to 2 hours, until doubled in volume.

5. **PRE-SHAPE AND BENCH REST:** On an unfloured surface, use the straight edge of the dough scraper to divide the dough into 8 pieces (about 100 grams each). Work the dough in your hands until it becomes a smooth ball. This dough is stiff, so this may take time. Leave the dough to rest for 10 to 20 minutes.

6. **PREPARE THE BAKING SHEETS:** Line two baking sheets with parchment paper and set aside.

7. **FINAL SHAPE:** Take a ball of dough and press a finger through the middle to create a hole. Rotate the bagel around your finger until the hole expands to 2 inches in diameter. Place the shaped bagel on the parchment paper. Repeat with the remaining balls of dough.

8. **PROOF:** Loosely cover the bagels with a cloth and proof at room temperature for 30 to 45 minutes.

9. **PREHEAT:** Preheat the oven to 500°F.

10. **POACHING:** Bring a large pot of water to a boil and add the baking soda. Add the bagels 1 to 3 at a time, making sure that none of the bagels overlap in the pot. Boil for 30 seconds. Flip the bagels over and boil for another 30 seconds. Transfer the poached bagels back to the parchment. Repeat with the remaining bagels.

11. **MAKE THE EGG WASH:** Beat together the egg and water and brush the egg wash over the surface of the bagels. Sprinkle ½ to 1 teaspoon of everything bagel seasoning on the top of each bagel.

12. **BAKE:** Place the bagels in the oven. If baking on separate racks, rotate the bagels halfway through the bake time for even baking. Reduce the temperature to 475°F and bake for 15 to 20 minutes, until browned.

13. **COOL:** Allow the bagels to cool on a cooling rack for 30 minutes before serving.

TIP: A way to see whether the bagels are proofed is to conduct a float test: Fill a bowl with room temperature water and put a bagel in the water. If it floats, the batch is ready. If it sinks, shake off the water and return it to the pan to proof longer.

BLACK SESAME STEAMED FLOWER BUNS

Yield : 10 large buns

PREP TIME: 45 TO 60 MINUTES | **INACTIVE TIME:** 3 TO 4 HOURS | **BAKE TIME:** 15 MINUTES

TOOLS NEEDED: small skillet, spice mill or small food processor or coffee grinder, food scale, large bowl, spoon, plastic dough scraper, parchment paper, 2-tier bamboo steamer, rolling pin, pastry brush, rolling pizza cutter, large wok or large pot with steaming adapter

Black sesame steamed flower buns are a uniquely flavored and uniquely shaped form of Chinese steamed buns. They are sweet with a slight nutty flavor. The color makes them a great bread to prepare for Moon Festival.

FOR THE DOUGH

20 grams black sesame seeds (2½ tablespoons)

200 grams warm water, divided (¾ cup plus 2 tablespoons)

50 grams white cane sugar (¼ cup)

4 grams instant yeast (1 teaspoon)

400 grams all-purpose flour (2⅔ cups)

12 grams lard, at room temperature (1 tablespoon)

5 grams baking powder (1 teaspoon)

2 grams salt (¼ teaspoon)

FOR SHAPING

2 tablespoons unsalted butter, at room temperature, or oil

1. **TOAST THE SESAME SEEDS:** Toast the black sesame seeds in a dry skillet for about 5 minutes over medium heat until fragrant, stirring frequently.

2. **GRIND THE SESAME SEEDS:** Grind the toasted black sesame seeds in a small food processor or coffee grinder until the texture looks like wet sand, the oils have released, and there are no more whole seeds. Set aside.

3. **WEIGH THE INGREDIENTS:** Making sure to tare after each addition, combine 190 grams of warm water, the sugar, and the instant yeast in a mixing bowl. Allow the

sugar to dissolve. Add the flour, lard, and baking powder.

4. **MIX:** Mix the ingredients together until a shaggy dough forms, then add 15 grams of ground black sesame seeds, the salt, and the remaining 10 grams of water. Mix to combine.

5. **KNEAD:** Turn the dough out onto a work surface and knead for 10 to 15 minutes by hand or 3 to 7 minutes with a dough hook in a stand mixer, until the dough is smooth, is no longer sticky, and releases easily from the bowl or work surface.

6. **BULK FERMENT:** Cover the dough and allow to ferment for 1½ to 2 hours, until doubled in volume.

7. **PREPARE THE STEAMER:** Place a round sheet of parchment made for bamboo steamers into the bottom of two bamboo steam trays.

8. **DIVIDE:** Divide the dough into 10 equal pieces (about 67 grams each). Roll each piece into a ball.

9. **SHAPE:** Use a rolling pin to flatten one ball into an oval that is 7½ to 8 inches long and 3½ to 4 inches wide. Brush with the butter. Using a rolling pizza cutter or knife, cut slits down the length of the oval that are ¼ inch apart, stopping ¼ inch from the edges of the dough so that it doesn't come apart. Turn the dough over. Roll up the dough at a slight diagonal angle along the length. Gently pull the edges to lengthen, then twist one end around the other side and press to the bottom of the bun to form a flower-shaped bun. Place on the prepared steam trays. Repeat with the remaining pieces. Place 5 shaped buns in each steam tray 2 inches apart and 1 inch from the sides of the tray.

10. **PROOF:** Stack the steam trays and place the cover on top. Proof in a warm place for 30 to 45 minutes, until the buns are at least 1½ times larger.

11. **BOIL THE WATER:** Fill a large wok with 2 to 3 inches of water. Bring to a boil.

12. **STEAM:** Place the closed bamboo steamer in the wok and steam for 15 minutes over high heat. After 12 minutes, rotate the trays for even steaming. The water level in the wok should be high enough so that the bottom of the steamer is submerged, but no higher than ¼ inch. After 15 minutes, turn off the heat and let the buns sit covered for 5 to 10 more minutes.

13. **SERVE.**

TIPS: *If lard is unavailable, oil, unsalted butter, or vegetable shortening can substitute. Buns can be re-steamed if they start to become dry. Steam over high heat for 2 to 3 minutes to soften them.*

HARVEST SEEDED WHOLE-WHEAT SOURDOUGH BREAD

Yield: 1 loaf

PREP TIME: 30 TO 45 MINUTES | **INACTIVE TIME:** 11½ TO 20 HOURS | **BAKE TIME:** 40 MINUTES

TOOLS NEEDED: food scale, 2 small bowls, pan or skillet, large bowl, spoon, plastic dough scraper, bread proofing bowl or colander lined with a kitchen towel, large Dutch oven or steam pan, parchment paper, bread lame or serrated bread knife, spray bottle, cooling rack

This combination of seeds, oats, honey, and whole wheat creates a delicious bread with an incredible texture. Enjoy this wholesome bread with butter alongside a fall family dinner, breakfast, or any ordinary mealtime.

FOR THE STARTER

15 grams sourdough starter (1 tablespoon)

60 grams water (¼ cup plus 3 tablespoons)

60 grams all-purpose flour (⅔ cup)

FOR THE DOUGH

370 grams water (1½ cups plus 1 tablespoon)

250 grams whole-wheat flour (1⅔ cups)

250 grams bread flour (1⅔ cups)

25 grams pumpkin seeds (¼ cup)

100 grams starter (about ½ cup)

11 grams sea salt (1½ teaspoons)

10 grams whole flaxseed or hulled sunflower seeds (1½ teaspoons)

Rice flour or semolina, for dusting the proofing bowl

FOR THE SOAKED OATS

30 grams quick oats (⅓ cup)

50 grams water (3½ tablespoons)

20 grams honey (1½ tablespoons)

1. **REFRESH THE STARTER:** About 6 to 10 hours before mixing your dough, stir together the sourdough starter with the water and the flour. Leave it at room temperature until it doubles in volume and becomes bubbly.

2. **MEASURE THE INGREDIENTS:** Place a large mixing bowl on the scale, tare, and pour in the water. Add the whole-wheat flour and bread flour.

3. **MIX:** Mix the ingredients together until no dry flour remains, either by hand or in a stand mixer using a dough hook on the lowest two speeds.

4. **AUTOLYSE:** Cover the bowl and let the dough rest for 20 minutes.

5. **SOAK THE OATS:** In a small bowl, mix the quick oats, water, and honey. Set this mixture aside to soak.

6. **TOAST THE PUMPKIN SEEDS:** Toast the pumpkin seeds over medium heat, stirring, until the seeds are slightly browned and they begin making popping sounds. Remove from the heat and set aside.

7. **ADD THE STARTER:** After the autolyse time is finished, place the bowl of dough on the scale. Add 100 grams of the starter and massage it into the dough.

8. **ADD THE SALT AND OATS:** Tare the weight of the dough, then add the salt and the soaked oats to the mixture. Massage them into the dough, rotating it and folding it to make sure everything is fully mixed in.

9. **ADD THE SEEDS:** Fold the cooled pumpkin seeds and flaxseed into the dough until well distributed.

10. **REST:** Cover and let the dough rest for 30 minutes.

11. **STRETCH AND FOLD:** Take the dough in hand one quarter at a time and pull the dough upward, then fold back into the middle. Repeat this process with the remaining three quarters. Cover the dough.

12. **BULK FERMENT:** Rest the dough at room temperature for 3 to 5 hours, until doubled in volume.

13. **PRE-SHAPE AND BENCH REST:** The dough should be smooth and pull away from the sides of the bowl. On an unfloured surface, quickly push the straight edge of a dough scraper under one half of the dough, then fold that half of the dough over itself. With the scraper, push under one side of the dough and rotate it in a circular motion with 3 to 5 turns until it's a round shape. Let the dough rest for 20 minutes.

14. **PREPARE THE PROOFING BOWL:** Dust your proofing bowl generously with rice flour, making sure to coat the sides well.

15. **FINAL SHAPE:** Flour the top of your dough. Push the straight edge of the dough scraper under the dough. Guiding with your opposite hand, flip the dough onto its floured side. Pick up the left and right edges of the dough, gently stretch outward, and fold the edges into the middle. Pinch together to seal the seam. Take the end of the dough below the seam and roll it onto itself in a spiral until it seals at the opposite end. The floured side should be facing up once again. Without flipping the dough over, use a scraper to rotate it in a circle

CONTINUED ON NEXT PAGE

until it has tightened into a ball. Quickly push the scraper under the dough and lift with your opposite hand, then flip the dough into the proofing bowl. The floured side should be down and the sticky side should be up. Cover.

16. **PROOF:** Proof for 1 to 2 hours at room temperature. The dough should rise up the sides of the bowl, and a finger pressed into it should leave an indentation.

17. **PREHEAT:** After 30 to 60 minutes of proofing, preheat your oven to 500°F with the Dutch oven inside on the center rack. If not using a Dutch oven, place a metal pan filled halfway with water on the lowest rack of the oven.

18. **BAKE:** Center an extra-long sheet of parchment paper over the proofing bowl. Holding the paper over the bowl by grasping the edges of the bowl, flip the bowl to turn the dough out. Use a bread lame to score the loaf with a slash across the top, about ¼ inch deep. Carefully pick up the edges of the parchment to transfer the dough into the preheated Dutch oven (or onto a baking sheet). Cover with the lid and place the bread in the oven. Spray the walls of the oven with water and shut the door. Reduce the oven temperature to 460°F and bake for 20 minutes. After 20 minutes, carefully remove the bread from the Dutch oven and place it directly on the oven rack. (Remove the steam pan if using manual steam.) Reduce the heat to 450°F and bake for an additional 20 minutes to create a golden-brown crust.

19. **COOL:** Cool for 1 hour on a cooling rack before serving.

HONEY, APPLE, AND RAISIN CHALLAH

Yield: 2 loaves

PREP TIME: 35 TO 45 MINUTES | **INACTIVE TIME:** 9 TO 16 HOURS | **BAKE TIME:** 30 TO 40 MINUTES

TOOLS NEEDED: food scale, food container, large bowl, spoon, plastic dough scraper, parchment paper, baking sheet, steam pan, small bowl, pastry brush, spray bottle, cooling rack

Rosh Hashanah is a time when we hope and pray for a year of sweetness. Breaking this challah with family and friends will certainly ensure a sweet time. Enjoy savoring this bread and sharing hope around the table.

FOR THE STARTER
30 grams sourdough starter (2 tablespoons) or ⅛ teaspoon instant yeast

15 grams white cane sugar (1 tablespoon)

50 grams water (3½ tablespoons)

100 grams all-purpose flour (⅔ cup)

FOR THE DOUGH
100 grams warm water, divided (about ½ cup)

3 grams instant yeast (1 teaspoon)

150 grams starter (about ¾ cup)

60 grams honey (3 tablespoons)

450 grams bread flour (3 cups)

50 grams whole-wheat flour (⅓ cup)

70 grams oil, such as olive oil or avocado oil (⅓ cup)

3 large eggs

10 grams salt (1½ teaspoons)

40 grams raisins (¼ cup)

70 grams Granny Smith apple, peeled and cut into ¼-inch pieces (½ cup)

FOR THE EGG WASH
1 large egg

⅛ teaspoon water

1 teaspoon sesame seeds (optional)

1. **MAKE THE STARTER:** About 8 to 12 hours before mixing your dough, combine the starter or yeast, sugar, water, and flour in a clean container. Cover and leave at room temperature. It will increase in volume and become bubbly.

2. **WEIGH THE INGREDIENTS:** Making sure to tare after each addition, combine 90 grams of warm water, the instant yeast, 150 grams of starter, the honey, bread flour, and whole-wheat flour in a mixing bowl.

3. **MIX:** Mix the ingredients together until a shaggy dough forms, then add the oil, eggs, salt, and the remaining 10 grams of water. Mix to combine.

CONTINUED ON NEXT PAGE

4. **FOLD:** Stretch and fold the dough for 3 to 5 minutes, until it develops some elasticity. Add the raisins and apple and continue folding for 5 to 10 more minutes or until the dough is smooth, is no longer sticky, and releases easily from the bowl or work surface. If you have a stand mixer, this step can be done with a dough hook for 3 to 7 minutes on the lowest two speeds.

5. **BULK FERMENT:** Cover the dough and ferment for 1½ to 3 hours, until doubled in volume.

6. **DIVIDE:** Divide the dough into four equal pieces for two medium loaves.

7. **PRE-SHAPE:** Line a baking sheet with parchment paper. Lightly flour your work surface, take a piece of dough, and roll it under your hands until it is about 12 inches long. Repeat with the remaining pieces of dough.

8. **SHAPE:** Take two lengths of dough and lay them side by side. Twist the ropes around each other two times. Then take the ends of the dough that are untwisted and fold them under, attaching them to the opposite ends to form a simple round challah shape. Repeat with the other two pieces of dough.

9. **PROOF:** Cover and proof for 45 to 75 minutes, until the loaves are about 1½ times larger in volume. Touching the dough should leave an indentation.

10. **PREHEAT:** Preheat the oven to 350°F. Place a steam pan filled with water on the lowest rack.

11. **MAKE THE EGG WASH:** Beat together the egg and water and brush the egg wash onto the challah. Sprinkle the sesame seeds over the top of the egg wash (if using).

12. **BAKE:** Place the challah in the oven and spray the walls of the oven with water. Bake for 25 minutes, then remove the steam pan and continue baking for 5 to 15 minutes longer, until the loaves are a shiny reddish brown.

13. **COOL:** Transfer the challah to a cooling rack and cool for 1 hour before serving.

TIP: Instant yeast can be omitted to create a naturally fermented bread. The fermentation and proofing stages will take 2 to 3 times longer using this method.

SKILLET CINNAMON-APPLE BREAD

Yield: 1 loaf (serves 8 to 12)

PREP TIME: 65 TO 70 MINUTES | **INACTIVE TIME:** 11 TO 15 HOURS | **BAKE TIME:** 30 TO 40 MINUTES

TOOLS NEEDED: food scale, food container, small pot, large bowl, spoon, plastic dough scraper, 10- to 12-inch cast-iron pan, knife, 2 small bowls, rolling pin, pizza cutter or bread knife, whisk

---

In our family, it's a joke to steal the center of someone's cinnamon roll. So naturally, the beautiful center of this bread goes missing quickly. These rolls are perfect for a fall brunch or Thanksgiving, but you can also swap the icing for vanilla ice cream to make a delicious dessert.

FOR THE STARTER

30 grams sourdough starter (2 tablespoons) or ⅛ teaspoon instant yeast

15 grams white cane sugar (1 tablespoon)

50 grams water (3½ tablespoons)

100 grams all-purpose flour (⅔ cup)

FOR THE DOUGH

120 grams milk (¼ cup and 3 tablespoons)

110 grams warm water, divided (¼ cup and 4 tablespoons)

43 grams unsalted butter, at room temperature, plus more for greasing the pan (3 tablespoons)

150 grams starter (about ¾ cup)

5 grams white cane sugar (1 teaspoon)

3 grams instant yeast (1 teaspoon) (may be omitted—see Focaccia Picnic Sandwiches tips on page 55)

400 grams bread flour (2¾ cups plus 1 tablespoon)

1 large egg yolk

8 grams sea salt (1¼ teaspoons)

FOR THE FILLING

1 Granny Smith apple

40 grams white cane sugar (3 tablespoons)

3 grams ground cinnamon (1 teaspoon)

Pinch ground cloves

14 grams unsalted butter, at room temperature (1 tablespoon)

FOR THE VANILLA ICING

65 grams powdered sugar (about ½ cup)

¼ teaspoon vanilla extract

1 to 3 teaspoons milk

28 grams unsalted butter, melted (2 tablespoons)

---

1. **MAKE THE STARTER:** About 8 to 12 hours before mixing your dough, combine the starter or yeast, sugar, water, and flour in a clean container. Cover and leave at room temperature. It will double in size and become bubbly.

CONTINUED ON NEXT PAGE

2. **WARM THE MILK:** Heat the milk until it reaches a temperature of 110°F to 120°F.

3. **WEIGH THE INGREDIENTS:** Making sure to tare after each addition, combine 100 grams of warm milk, 100 grams of warm water, and the butter in a mixing bowl. Add 150 grams of starter, the sugar, the instant yeast, and the flour.

4. **MIX:** Mix the ingredients together until a shaggy dough forms, then add the egg yolk, remaining 10 grams of water, and salt. Mix.

5. **KNEAD:** Turn the dough out onto a work surface and knead for 10 to 15 minutes by hand or 3 to 7 minutes with a dough hook in a stand mixer on the lowest two speeds, until the dough is smooth, is no longer sticky, and releases easily from the bowl.

6. **BULK FERMENT:** Cover the dough and ferment for 1½ to 2 hours, until doubled in volume.

7. **PREPARE THE BAKING DISH:** Rub butter on the inside of a 10- to 12-inch cast-iron skillet or pie dish. Sprinkle a light coating of flour over the butter.

8. **PREPARE THE FILLING:** Peel the apple, then cut it into thin strips that are ¹⁄₁₆ to ⅛ inch thick and about 1 inch wide. In a separate bowl, mix the sugar, cinnamon, and cloves together.

9. **SHAPE:** Place the dough on a lightly floured work surface. Dust flour onto a rolling pin and roll the dough into a 12-inch square that is ½ inch thick. Rub the butter onto the dough until it is completely covered.

Evenly sprinkle all the cinnamon-sugar mixture onto the dough. With a pizza cutter or bread knife, cut the dough vertically into 12 (1-inch wide) strips. Starting with the center strips, place them cut-side down in the center of the pan and curl into a loose spiral with the cinnamon sugar-coated side facing inward. There should be about ¼ inch of room left between the spiraled strip layers for expansion and the apples. Repeat with the next strip, pinch the ends together, and continue the spiral. Continue with the remaining strips of dough, creating one large spiral roll. Pinch the end of the final strip to the outside of the spiral to close the pattern. Starting at the center of the spiral, place apple slices between every layer until it is filled.

10. **PROOF:** Cover and proof for 45 to 75 minutes. The dough should be larger in volume and leave an indentation when tested with a fingertip.

11. **PREHEAT:** Preheat the oven to 375°F.

12. **BAKE:** Place the pan in the oven and bake for 30 to 40 minutes. Check the bread after 20 minutes and tent with aluminum foil if the top is browning too quickly.

13. **COOL:** Let the bread cool for 20 minutes before icing.

14. **PREPARE THE ICING:** Whisk together the powdered sugar, vanilla, milk, and butter. Use a spoon to drizzle the icing over the bread.

15. **SERVING:** Cut into slices and serve.

BAGUETTE ROLLS

Yield: 8 medium-size rolls

PREP TIME: 25 TO 40 MINUTES | **INACTIVE TIME:** 11½ TO 20 HOURS
BAKE TIME: 18 TO 20 MINUTES PER BATCH

TOOLS NEEDED: food scale, large bowl, spoon, plastic dough scraper, 2 baking sheets, parchment paper, steam pan, bread lame or serrated bread knife, spray bottle, cooling rack

Baguette rolls have simple ingredients but amazing flavor, especially with fresh butter or olive oil. The long fermentation of sourdough makes the flavor complex and satisfying. They are festive for a Thanksgiving dinner or family event, and they're also perfect for making rustic sandwiches.

FOR THE STARTER
15 grams sourdough starter
(1 tablespoon) or
⅛ teaspoon instant yeast

60 grams water (¼ cup
plus 3 tablespoons)

60 grams all-purpose
flour (⅔ cup)

FOR THE DOUGH
330 grams water, divided
(1⅓ cups plus
1 tablespoon)

100 grams whole-wheat
flour (⅔ cup)

400 grams bread flour (2⅔ cups)

100 grams starter
(about ½ cup)

10 grams sea salt
(1½ teaspoons)

1. **REFRESH THE STARTER:** About 6 to 10 hours before mixing your dough, stir together the starter or yeast, water, and flour. Leave at room temperature until it doubles in volume and becomes bubbly.

2. **WEIGH THE INGREDIENTS:** Making sure to tare after each addition, combine 320 grams of water, the whole-wheat flour, and the bread flour in a mixing bowl.

3. **MIX:** Using a spoon, mix the ingredients together. (If using a stand mixer and a dough hook, mix on the lowest two speeds for 2 to 5 minutes.)

4. **AUTOLYSE:** Cover the bowl and let the dough rest for 20 minutes.

5. **ADD THE STARTER:** Tare the weight of the bowl and add 100 grams of starter. Massage the starter into the dough until distributed throughout.

6. **ADD THE SALT:** Tare the bowl, add the salt, then very slowly pour the remaining 10 grams of water over the salt to dissolve. Massage the salt and water into the dough, rotating and folding to make sure it is fully mixed in.

CONTINUED ON NEXT PAGE

7. **KNEAD:** Turn the dough out onto a work surface and knead for 5 to 10 minutes by hand or 3 to 6 minutes with a dough hook in a stand mixer on the lowest two speeds.

8. **BULK FERMENT:** Let the dough ferment at room temperature for 4 to 7 hours, until doubled in volume.

9. **DIVIDE:** The fermented dough should look smooth, be larger in volume with bubbles, and pull away from the sides of the bowl easily. Transfer it to an unfloured surface and divide it using the sharp edge of the dough scraper into 8 pieces (about 116 grams each).

10. **PRE-SHAPE AND BENCH REST:** Take a piece of dough and, using the dough scraper, fold one half of the dough over the top and rotate the dough in a circle until it has a smooth appearance and round shape. Repeat with the remaining pieces of dough. Leave the dough to rest for 20 minutes.

11. **PREPARE THE BAKING SHEETS:** Line two baking sheets with parchment paper and set aside.

12. **FINAL SHAPE:** Flour the work surface and the top of one of the pre-shaped pieces of dough. Push the straight edge of the dough scraper under the dough and flip it over. Use your hands to flatten the dough into a ½- to 1-inch-thick square shape. Take the top two corners and fold them into the middle at right angles to create a triangle shape at the top of the dough. Next, take the triangle top of the dough and fold it down to touch the bottom. Fold the left and right sides of the dough into the center to touch the edges of the triangle. Pick up the top half of the dough, fold it down to the bottom half, and pinch the edges together into a seam. Finally, roll the dough back and forth under your hands, gently pulling outward as you roll, stretching the dough to about 5 inches long. The dough should be thicker in the middle with tapered edges. Transfer to one of the prepared baking sheets, seam-side down. Repeat with the remaining pieces of dough, spacing them 3 inches apart on the baking sheets.

13. **PROOF:** Proof the baguette rolls uncovered for 30 to 60 minutes at room temperature. Loosely cover the rolls and place the baking sheets in the refrigerator for 30 to 60 minutes to firm the dough while the oven preheats.

14. **PREHEAT:** Preheat the oven to 500°F and place a steam pan filled with water on the lowest rack.

15. **BAKE:** Remove the first baking sheet from the refrigerator and cut a score down the middle of the rolls about ¼ inch deep, then place the baking sheet in the hot oven. Quickly spray water on the oven walls and

close the door. Reduce the temperature to 475°F and bake for 12 minutes. Remove the steam pan and bake for 6 to 8 minutes longer, until the crust hardens and develops a golden-brown color. Repeat this step with the other baking sheet of baguette rolls.

16. **COOL:** Cool the rolls for 30 minutes on a cooling rack before serving.

TIPS: To substitute commercial yeast for the sourdough starter, combine 60 grams of flour, 60 grams of water, and ⅛ teaspoon of instant yeast. Add 3 grams of additional instant yeast in step 2. Adjust the time needed for the bulk ferment to 1½ to 3 hours and proofing to 30 to 90 minutes. To adjust the timing to your schedule, you can refrigerate the dough during the bulk fermentation process, leaving the dough to ferment for 24 to 48 hours.

Mushroom Baozi, page 128

Chapter Five
WINTER

In winter, we turn toward spices, strong flavors, and enriched breads as we gather with the people we love to celebrate special holidays and fill this dark season with light.

GINGERBREAD SCONES WITH EGGNOG ICING

Yield : 8 large scones

PREP TIME: 30 MINUTES | **INACTIVE TIME:** 30 TO 65 MINUTES | **BAKE TIME:** 18 TO 22 MINUTES

TOOLS NEEDED: 2 baking sheets, parchment paper, food scale, mixing bowl, spoon, pastry cutter or two forks, rolling pin, small bowl, whisk, butter knife

All the best flavors of the holiday season come together in these gingerbread scones with eggnog icing. These scones are sweet and spicy with a softer texture. They are the perfect combination of a soft gingerbread cookie and a scone.

FOR THE DOUGH
350 grams all-purpose flour (2⅓ cups)

50 grams whole-wheat flour (⅓ cup)

150 grams white cane sugar (¾ cup)

50 grams brown sugar (¼ cup)

15 grams baking powder (1 tablespoon)

4 grams salt (½ teaspoon)

6 grams ground ginger (2 teaspoons)

3 grams ground cinnamon (1 teaspoon)

1 gram ground nutmeg (¼ teaspoon)

1 gram ground cloves (¼ teaspoon)

157 grams unsalted butter, cold (½ cup plus 3 tablespoons)

100 grams whole milk, chilled (7 tablespoons)

75 grams molasses (¼ cup)

1 large egg

FOR THE EGGNOG ICING
160 grams powdered sugar (about 2½ cups)

2 to 3 tablespoons whole milk

2 teaspoons ground nutmeg (freshly ground, if possible)

2 tablespoons unsalted butter, at room temperature

1. **PREPARE THE BAKING SHEETS:** Line two baking sheets with parchment paper.
2. **WEIGH THE INGREDIENTS:** Making sure to tare after each addition, combine the all-purpose flour, whole-wheat flour, white sugar, brown sugar, baking powder, salt, ginger, cinnamon, nutmeg, and cloves in a mixing bowl. Mix well to combine.
3. **ADD THE BUTTER:** Cut the cold butter in half, then cut each half into eight pieces and add to the dry mixture. With two forks or a pastry cutter, cut the butter into smaller pieces and distribute throughout the dough until crumbly and sandy. Some big pieces are okay, but there should be no pieces bigger than a pea.
4. **MIX:** Add the chilled milk, molasses, and egg. Stir until there are no longer any patches of dry flour. Don't overmix or add extra milk; this dough takes time to come together.

5. **CHILL:** Chill the dough for 10 to 30 minutes before shaping.

6. **PREHEAT:** Preheat the oven to 400°F.

7. **SHAPE:** Turn the dough out onto a floured work surface. Quickly pat down the top and edges. With a rolling pin, roll the dough into an 8-inch square that is 1 inch thick.

8. **DIVIDE:** Divide the dough into quarters, then cut each quarter diagonally to create 8 large wedges. Place the wedges on the prepared baking sheets at least 2 inches apart. If they are softening, chill for 10 to 30 minutes before baking.

9. **BAKE:** Bake for 18 to 22 minutes, until the edges are just starting to turn brown and a toothpick inserted comes out clean.

10. **COOL:** Cool for 10 to 30 minutes, until just warm.

11. **ICE AND SERVE:** Whisk the powdered sugar, milk, nutmeg, and butter together. Place 1 to 2 tablespoons of icing on top of the scone, then spread with a butter knife. Let the icing harden for 10 to 15 minutes.

12. **SERVE.**

TIP: Scones can be frozen before baking and baked straight from the freezer, with 3 to 8 additional minutes of baking time.

MANDARIN, OLIVE OIL, AND POPPY SEED QUICK BREAD

Yield: 1 loaf

PREP TIME: 20 MINUTES | **INACTIVE TIME:** 20 MINUTES | **BAKE TIME:** 50 TO 60 MINUTES

TOOLS NEEDED: food scale, 2 mixing bowls, zester, juicing tool, spoon, loaf pan, parchment paper, spatula, knife, small bowl, whisk

The rich flavors of citrus, olive oil, and poppy seeds give this bread a beautiful earthy flavor that isn't overly sweet. The sweet glaze gives it a nice finishing touch for sharing with others.

FOR THE DOUGH

225 grams
all-purpose flour (1½ cups)

75 grams whole-wheat
flour (½ cup)

15 grams baking powder
(1 tablespoon)

3 grams salt (½ teaspoon)

230 grams whole milk (1 cup)

1 large egg

115 grams white cane sugar
(½ cup plus 1 tablespoon)

65 grams extra-virgin
olive oil (⅓ cup)

4 grams mandarin zest
(2 teaspoons, from 1 or
2 small mandarins)

30 grams freshly squeezed
mandarin juice (2 tablespoons)

5 grams poppy seeds
(2 teaspoons)

FOR THE GLAZE

65 grams powdered
sugar (½ cup)

1 to 3 teaspoons freshly
squeezed mandarin juice

1. **PREHEAT:** Preheat the oven to 350°F.
2. **MIX THE DRY INGREDIENTS:** Stir together the all-purpose flour, whole-wheat flour, baking powder, and salt in a mixing bowl.
3. **MIX THE WET INGREDIENTS:** In a separate bowl, combine the milk, egg, sugar, olive oil, mandarin zest, mandarin juice, and poppy seeds. Stir well.
4. **COMBINE:** Pour the wet mixture into the dry mixture. Stir together until combined, making sure not to overmix.
5. **PREPARE THE LOAF PAN:** Line a loaf pan with parchment (see step 6 of Zucchini Bread on page 44) or grease a loaf pan.
6. **FILL THE LOAF PAN:** Use a spatula to transfer the dough to the prepared pan.
7. **BAKE:** Bake for 50 to 60 minutes. The bread should have a golden-brown top, and a knife inserted in the center should come out clean.
8. **COOL:** Cool for about 20 minutes.
9. **GLAZE AND SERVE:** Whisk together the glaze and drizzle over the cooled bread. Serve.

SWEET PEPPER CORN BREAD

Yield: 1 loaf (serves 9 to 12)

PREP TIME: 30 TO 35 MINUTES | **INACTIVE TIME:** 20 MINUTES | **BAKE TIME:** 35 TO 40 MINUTES

TOOLS NEEDED: food scale, large bowl, spoon, cutting board, knife, saucepan, 8-inch square baking pan, spatula

---

This corn bread is smoky and sweet with a beautiful texture. Sweet pepper corn bread can be delicious any time of year, but it makes a great addition to a Kwanzaa meal. The peppers used can be red, green, or a combination to represent the traditional colors of Kwanzaa.

FOR THE DOUGH

32 grams unsalted butter, melted, divided (3 tablespoons)

255 grams buttermilk (1 cup plus 5 teaspoons) (see step 3 of Irish-Inspired Soda Bread on page 16 for how to substitute whole milk)

240 grams cornmeal (1¼ cups plus 2½ tablespoons)

150 grams whole-wheat flour (1 cup)

70 grams avocado oil (⅓ cup)

60 grams honey (¼ cup)

1 large egg

4 grams chili powder (1 teaspoon)

3 grams salt (½ teaspoon)

2 grams baking soda (½ teaspoon)

70 grams red or green bell pepper, cut into ¼-inch pieces (heaping ⅓ cup)

1. **PREHEAT:** Preheat the oven to 350°F.
2. **WEIGH THE INGREDIENTS:** Tare a large mixing bowl, then combine 28 grams of butter, the buttermilk, cornmeal, flour, oil, honey, egg, chili powder, salt, and baking soda in the mixing bowl.
3. **MIX:** Mix the ingredients together until a thick batter forms and there are no dry areas of flour left in the bowl.
4. **ADD THE CHOPPED PEPPERS:** Fold the pepper pieces into the batter.
5. **PREPARE THE BAKING DISH:** Use the remaining 5 grams of melted butter to grease an 8-inch square baking pan.
6. **FILL THE BAKING DISH:** Use a spatula to scrape the corn bread batter into the baking dish.
7. **BAKE:** Place the pan in the oven and bake for 35 to 40 minutes. Check the pan after 20 minutes and tent with aluminum foil if the top is browning too quickly. The bread should have a golden-brown top, and a toothpick or knife inserted into the center should come out clean.
8. **COOL AND SERVE:** Allow to cool for about 20 minutes, then cut into squares and serve.

CHRISTMAS TREE TEAR-AND-SHARE ROLLS

Yield : 23 rolls

PREP TIME: 45 TO 50 MINUTES | **INACTIVE TIME:** 11 TO 15 HOURS | **BAKE TIME:** 20 TO 25 MINUTES

TOOLS NEEDED: food scale, 2 large bowls, spoon, plastic dough scraper, 2 small saucepans, baking sheet, parchment paper

---

It doesn't get much more festive than rolls baked in the shape of a Christmas tree. Although it's a bit on-the-nose for adults but fun for kids, everyone will agree that these garlic butter rolls are delicious.

FOR THE STARTER
15 grams sourdough starter (1 tablespoon) or ⅛ teaspoon instant yeast

110 grams water (7½ tablespoons)

110 grams all-purpose flour (¾ cup)

FOR THE DOUGH
80 grams milk (⅓ cup)

110 grams warm water, divided (7½ tablespoons)

200 grams starter (about 1 cup)

5 grams white cane sugar (1 teaspoon)

4 grams instant yeast (1 teaspoon)

28 grams unsalted butter, at room temperature (2 tablespoons)

340 grams all-purpose flour (2¼ cups)

40 grams whole-wheat flour (⅓ cup)

8 grams salt (1¼ teaspoons)

FOR THE TOPPING
32 grams unsalted butter (3 tablespoons)

2 garlic cloves, minced

Fresh rosemary, for garnish

1. **MAKE THE STARTER:** About 8 to 12 hours before mixing your dough, combine the starter or yeast, water, and flour in a bowl. Mix well, cover, and leave at room temperature in a warm place until bubbly and doubled in volume.

2. **WARM THE MILK:** Heat the milk until it reaches a temperature of 110°F to 120°F.

3. **WEIGH THE INGREDIENTS:** Tare a large mixing bowl and combine 70 grams of warm milk, 100 grams of warm water, 200 grams of starter, the sugar, and the instant yeast. Add the butter, all-purpose flour, and whole-wheat flour.

4. **MIX:** Mix the ingredients together until a shaggy dough forms, then add the salt and remaining 10 grams of water. Mix to combine.

5. **KNEAD:** Turn the dough out onto a work surface and knead for 10 to 15 minutes by hand or 3 to 7 minutes with a dough hook in a stand mixer on the lowest two speeds, until the dough is smooth, is no longer sticky, and releases easily from the bowl or work surface.

6. **BULK FERMENT:** Cover the dough and allow to ferment for 1½ to 2 hours, until doubled in volume.
7. **PREPARE THE BAKING SHEET:** Line a flat baking sheet with parchment paper and set aside.
8. **DIVIDE:** Divide the dough into 23 equal pieces (about 34 grams each).
9. **SHAPE:** Take a piece of dough and flatten it into a disc. Gather the edges into the center and pinch together to make a seam. Turn the dough over onto the seam and rotate briskly under your palm into a tight ball. Repeat with the remaining pieces of dough.
10. **ARRANGE THE TREE:** The tree will consist of 7 rows; 1 roll on row 1, 2 rolls on row 2, etc. You will have 2 rolls for row 7 to form the stump.
11. **PROOF:** Cover and proof in a warm place for 45 to 60 minutes, until the rolls are puffy and pressing into one another.
12. **PREHEAT:** Preheat the oven to 375°F.
13. **BAKE:** Place the baking sheet in the preheated oven. Bake for 20 to 25 minutes, until the rolls are golden brown.
14. **MAKE THE GARLIC BUTTER:** While the rolls are baking, in a small saucepan, melt the butter. Add the minced garlic and sauté until fragrant and translucent. Turn off the heat and set aside. As soon as the rolls come out of the oven, pour the garlic butter over the top.
15. **COOL:** Let the rolls cool and soak in the butter for 10 to 15 minutes.
16. **GARNISH AND SERVE:** Garnish with rosemary and serve on a large charcuterie board, pan, or fresh sheet of parchment as a centerpiece.

TIP: Instant yeast can be omitted to create a naturally fermented bread. The fermentation and proofing process will take 2 to 3 times longer.

BAKED BRIE TEAR-AND-SHARE WREATH

Yield: 24 rolls

PREP TIME: 45 TO 50 MINUTES | **INACTIVE TIME:** 11 TO 15 HOURS | **BAKE TIME:** 20 TO 24 MINUTES

TOOLS NEEDED: food scale, food container, large bowl, spoon, 2 small saucepans, plastic dough scraper, baking sheet, parchment paper, knife, small bowl, pastry brush, serving plate, butter knife

---

This baked Brie tear-and-share wreath looks beautiful on the serving table and makes a great appetizer and conversation starter at a party. This bread is the perfect invitation to gather and break bread.

FOR THE STARTER

15 grams sourdough starter (1 tablespoon) or ⅛ teaspoon instant yeast

110 grams water (7½ tablespoons)

110 grams all-purpose flour (¾ cup)

FOR THE DOUGH

115 grams milk (¼ cup plus 2½ tablespoons)

150 grams warm water, divided (⅔ cup)

200 grams starter (about 1 cup)

5 grams white cane sugar (1 teaspoon)

6 grams instant yeast (1½ teaspoons) (may be omitted, see the Christmas Tree Tear-and-Share Rolls tip on page 107)

500 grams all-purpose flour (3½ cups)

50 grams whole-wheat flour (⅓ cup)

10 grams salt (1½ teaspoons)

42 grams unsalted butter, at room temperature (3 tablespoons)

1 round Brie cheese, chilled

FOR THE EGG WASH

1 large egg

¼ teaspoon water

Pinch salt

Fresh rosemary, for garnish

1. **MAKE THE STARTER:** About 8 to 12 hours before mixing your dough, mix together the starter or yeast, water, and flour. Cover and leave at room temperature in a warm place until bubbly and doubled in volume.

2. **WARM THE MILK:** Heat the milk until it reaches a temperature of 110°F to 120°F.

3. **WEIGH THE INGREDIENTS:** Tare a large mixing bowl and combine 100 grams of warm milk and 140 grams of warm water. Add 200 grams of starter, the sugar, instant yeast, all-purpose flour, and whole-wheat flour.

4. **MIX:** Mix the ingredients together until a shaggy dough forms, then add the salt and remaining 10 grams of water. Mix to combine.

5. **ADD BUTTER:** Fold the butter into the dough.

6. **KNEAD:** Turn the dough out onto a work surface and knead for 10 to 15 minutes by hand or 3 to 7 minutes with a dough hook in a stand mixer on the lowest two speeds, until the dough is smooth, is no longer sticky, and releases easily from the bowl or work surface.

7. **BULK FERMENT:** Cover the dough and ferment for 1½ to 2 hours, until doubled in volume.

8. **PREPARE THE BAKING SHEET:** Line a baking sheet with parchment paper and set aside.

9. **DIVIDE:** For a 3-inch round of Brie, divide the dough into 24 equal pieces (about 44 grams each). For a larger round, see the tips at the end of this recipe.

10. **SHAPE:** Take a piece of dough and flatten it into a disc. Gather the edges into the center and pinch together to make a seam. Turn the dough over and rotate briskly under your palm to form a tight ball. Repeat with the remaining pieces of dough.

11. **ARRANGE THE WREATH:** Unwrap your Brie and place it in the center of the parchment. Place 8 of the rolls around the cheese, evenly spaced and just touching the cheese. Arrange the remaining 16 rolls around the first ring, leaving about ¼ inch between the rolls.

12. **PROOF:** Cover and proof in a warm place for 30 to 60 minutes, until the rolls are puffy and pressing into one another.

13. **PREHEAT:** Preheat the oven to 375°F.

14. **MAKE THE EGG WASH:** Beat together the egg, water, and salt and brush onto the tops of the rolls.

15. **BAKE:** Place the rolls in the oven and bake for 20 to 24 minutes, until the rolls are golden brown.

16. **COOL:** Allow the rolls to cool for 5 to 10 minutes at room temperature.

17. **GARNISH AND SERVE:** Transfer the wreath to a large serving plate, platter, or cutting board. Garnish with sprigs of rosemary. Place a butter knife into the Brie for people to serve the melted Brie onto their plates.

TIPS: For a 5- to 6-inch round of Brie, divide the dough into 27 pieces for an inner ring of 9 rolls and an outer ring of 18 rolls.
If prepping in advance, the wreath can be proofed in the refrigerator for 4 to 8 hours.

ORANGE KNOTS

Yield: 16 knots

PREP TIME: 45 TO 65 MINUTES | **INACTIVE TIME:** 12½ TO 18½ HOURS | **BAKE TIME:** 18 TO 20 MINUTES

TOOLS NEEDED: food scale, food container, small saucepan, large bowl, zester, juicing tool, spoon, plastic dough scraper, baking sheet, parchment paper, small bowl, whisk, teaspoon

Orange knots are filled with flavor and will brighten up the gloomiest winter days. These are excellent as a morning pastry or with some afternoon tea. The crisp flavor and creamy texture of the glaze make them an incredible treat!

FOR THE STARTER
30 grams sourdough starter (2 tablespoons)

70 grams water (⅓ cup)

18 grams white cane sugar (1 tablespoon)

120 grams all-purpose flour (¾ cup plus 1 tablespoon)

FOR THE DOUGH
220 grams whole milk (¾ cup plus 2 tablespoons)

50 grams white cane sugar (¼ cup)

200 grams starter (about 1 cup)

325 grams all-purpose flour (2 cups plus 3 tablespoons)

75 grams whole-wheat flour (½ cup)

8 grams orange zest (about 2 teaspoons)

50 grams freshly squeezed orange juice (3½ tablespoons)

8 grams salt (1¼ teaspoons)

56 grams unsalted butter, at room temperature (4 tablespoons)

FOR THE GLAZE
7 grams unsalted butter, at room temperature (½ tablespoon)

100 grams powdered sugar (⅞ cup)

4 to 8 grams freshly squeezed orange juice (1 to 2 teaspoons)

1. **MAKE THE STARTER:** About 8 to 12 hours before mixing your dough, mix together the starter, water, sugar, and flour. Cover and let the yeast activate until the starter has doubled in volume and is bubbly.

2. **WARM THE MILK:** Heat the milk until it reaches a temperature of 115°F to 120°F.

3. **WEIGH THE INGREDIENTS:** Tare a large mixing bowl, then combine 200 grams of warm milk, the sugar, and 200 grams of starter. Allow the sugar to dissolve. Add the all-purpose flour, whole-wheat flour, and orange zest.

4. **MIX:** Mix the ingredients together until a shaggy dough forms, then add the orange juice and salt. Mix to combine.

5. **ADD THE BUTTER:** Slowly add the butter in two stages, mixing after each addition.

6. **KNEAD:** Turn the dough out onto a work surface and knead for 10 to 15 minutes by hand or 3 to 8 minutes with a dough hook in a stand mixer on the lowest two speeds, until the dough is smooth, is no longer sticky, and releases easily from the bowl or work surface.

7. **BULK FERMENT:** Cover the dough and ferment for 3 to 4 hours, until doubled in volume.

8. **PREPARE THE BAKING SHEET:** Line a large baking sheet with parchment paper and set aside.

9. **SHAPE:** Divide the dough into 16 equal pieces (about 53 grams each). Roll a piece of dough under your hands to form an 11-inch rope. Take the ends and tie a simple knot in the center. Then tuck the ends of the rope under and pinch to seal to the underside of the knot. Repeat with the remaining pieces of dough. Place the knots 2 to 3 inches apart on the baking sheet.

10. **PROOF:** Cover and proof in a warm place for 1½ to 2½ hours, until the knots are fuller in volume and gently pressing the dough with your finger leaves an indentation.

11. **PREHEAT:** Preheat the oven to 375°F.

12. **BAKE:** Bake for 18 to 20 minutes, until golden brown.

13. **MAKE THE GLAZE:** While the knots are baking, whisk together the butter, powdered sugar, and orange juice into a thick consistency.

14. **GLAZE AND COOL:** Scoop a heaping teaspoon of glaze on top of each knot while still warm so that the glaze melts down the edges—it will set as they cool. Cool the knots for about 10 minutes, then serve.

TIP: You can add 1 teaspoon of instant yeast in step 3 with the sugar and starter if you'd like to speed up the bulk fermentation. The fermentation will take 1½ to 2 hours with this addition, and the proofing time will be 45 to 75 minutes.

CHAI-SPICED STAR BREAD

Yield: 1 large shaped loaf (serves 8 to 12)

PREP TIME: 50 TO 60 MINUTES | **INACTIVE TIME:** 10½ TO 15½ HOURS
BAKE TIME: 30 TO 35 MINUTES

TOOLS NEEDED: food scale, bowl, small saucepan, large bowl, spoon, plastic dough scraper, small bowl, baking sheet, parchment paper, rolling pin, spatula, circle biscuit cutter, sharp knife

---

In wintertime, enjoy this chai-spiced star bread for breakfast or dessert for a special weekend, winter solstice, or Christmas. I love the crisp outside and chewy interior of this bread and, of course, the spicy flavors!

FOR THE STARTER
15 grams sourdough starter
(1 tablespoon) or
⅛ teaspoon instant yeast
110 grams water (½ cup)
110 grams all-purpose flour
(⅔ cup plus 1 tablespoon)

FOR THE DOUGH
190 grams whole milk
(¾ cup plus 2 teaspoons)
4 grams instant yeast
(1 teaspoon)
15 grams white cane
sugar (1 tablespoon)

200 grams starter (about 1 cup)
28 grams unsalted butter,
at room temperature
(2 tablespoons)
380 grams all-purpose
flour (2⅔ cups)
1 large egg yolk
8 grams salt (1 teaspoon)
Powdered sugar, for
topping (optional)

FOR THE FILLING
160 grams unsalted butter,
at room temperature
(½ cup plus 7 tablespoons)

60 grams brown sugar
(¼ cup plus 1 tablespoon)
4 grams ground
cinnamon (1 teaspoon)
2 grams ground ginger
(½ teaspoon)
2 grams ground cloves
(½ teaspoon)
2 grams ground cardamom
(½ teaspoon)
Pinch freshly ground black
pepper (optional)

1. **MAKE THE STARTER:** About 8 to 12 hours before mixing your dough, mix the starter or yeast, water, and flour together in a bowl. Cover and let activate until bubbly and doubled in volume.
2. **WARM THE MILK:** Heat the milk until it reaches a temperature of 115°F to 120°F.
3. **WEIGH THE INGREDIENTS:** Tare a mixing bowl, then combine 180 grams of warm milk, the

instant yeast, the sugar, and 200 grams of starter. Allow the sugar to dissolve. Add the butter and flour.
4. **MIX:** Mix the ingredients until a shaggy dough forms, then add the egg yolk and salt. Mix to combine.

CONTINUED ON NEXT PAGE

5. **KNEAD:** Turn the dough out onto a work surface and knead for 10 to 15 minutes by hand or 3 to 7 minutes with a dough hook in a stand mixer on the lowest two speeds, until the dough is smooth, is no longer sticky, and releases easily from the bowl or work surface.

6. **BULK FERMENT:** Cover the dough and ferment for 1½ to 2 hours, until doubled in volume.

7. **PREPARE THE FILLING:** Mix together the butter, brown sugar, cinnamon, ginger, cloves, cardamom, and black pepper (if using) in a small bowl until it forms a smooth mixture.

8. **DIVIDE:** Divide the dough into four equal pieces. Roll each quarter into a rough ball.

9. **PREPARE THE BAKING SHEET:** Line a large baking sheet with parchment paper and set aside.

10. **ROLL AND FILL THE LAYERS OF DOUGH:** Place one of the quarters of dough on a lightly floured work surface. Roll the dough into a 12-inch circle and place on the prepared baking sheet. Spread one-third of the filling mixture over the dough, leaving a 1-inch margin. Roll out the second quarter of dough into a 12-inch circle and carefully place it over the first piece. Press the edges together to seal. Spread the next third of the filling over the dough, again reserving the 1-inch margin. Repeat with the third piece of dough and the final third of filling. Roll out the final quarter of dough in the same way and place it on top. Seal the edges together.

11. **SHAPE:** Place a 2- to 3-inch diameter circular biscuit cutter in the center of the top circle (do not press down). Use a sharp knife to cut equally spaced lines radiating from the edge of the cutter. Cut into quarters first, then divide each quarter into four smaller sections until 16 cuts are made around the diameter of the dough. Pick up two strips of dough and twist away from each other two times. Press the ends of the strips together into a point. Pick up the next two pieces next to the twisted pair and repeat. Continue moving around the dough until you have an 8-point star shape. Remove the circular biscuit cutter from the top of the dough.

12. **PROOF:** Cover and proof in a warm place for 30 to 60 minutes, until the layers are puffy.

13. **PREHEAT:** Preheat the oven to 365°F.

14. **BAKE:** Bake for 30 to 35 minutes, until the crust is golden brown and the filling is bubbling.

15. **COOL:** Let the loaf cool for 20 to 30 minutes.

16. **SERVE:** Transfer to a serving platter or clean baking sheet, cut into wedges, and serve. Dust lightly with powdered sugar, if desired.

TIP: Instant yeast can be omitted to create a naturally fermented bread. The fermentation and proofing stages will take about 2 to 3 times longer using this method.

ST. NICHOLAS MINI BABKAS

Yield: 8 small babkas

PREP TIME: 45 TO 60 MINUTES | **INACTIVE TIME:** 9½ TO 15 HOURS
BAKE TIME: 20 TO 24 MINUTES PER BATCH

TOOLS NEEDED: food scale, food container, small pot, large bowl, zester, spoon, plastic dough scraper, 2 baking sheets, parchment paper, glass bowl, rolling pin, pastry brush, serrated bread knife, cooling rack

In early December, many people observe the Feast of St. Nicholas by leaving gifts like coins, chocolate, or oranges to symbolize the gold St. Nicholas gave to people in need. These mini babkas with orange zest and chocolate filling are a festive way to begin the day.

FOR THE STARTER
15 grams sourdough starter (1 tablespoon) or ⅛ teaspoon instant yeast

60 grams water (¼ cup plus 3 tablespoons)

60 grams all-purpose flour (⅔ cup)

FOR THE DOUGH
130 grams whole milk (½ cup)

100 grams starter (about ½ cup)

60 grams white cane sugar (4 tablespoons)

4 grams instant yeast (1 teaspoon)

500 grams all-purpose flour (3½ cups plus 1 tablespoon)

Zest of 1 orange

28 grams unsalted butter, melted (2 tablespoons)

6 grams salt (1 teaspoon)

FOR THE FILLING
50 grams semisweet chocolate chips (¼ cup)

28 grams unsalted butter, at room temperature (2 tablespoons)

60 grams white cane sugar (4 tablespoons)

1. **MAKE THE STARTER:** About 6 to 10 hours before mixing your dough, combine the starter or yeast, water, and flour in a clean container. Cover and leave at room temperature until doubled in volume and bubbly.

2. **WARM THE MILK:** Heat the milk until it reaches a temperature of 110°F to 120°F.

3. **WEIGH THE INGREDIENTS:** Tare a mixing bowl, then combine 120 grams of warm milk, 100 grams of starter, the sugar, and the instant yeast. Allow the sugar to dissolve. Add the flour and the orange zest.

4. **MIX:** Mix the ingredients together until a shaggy dough is formed, then add the melted butter and the salt. Mix to combine.

5. **KNEAD:** Turn the dough out onto a work surface and knead for 10 to 15 minutes by hand or 4 to 8 minutes with a dough hook in a stand mixer on the lowest two speeds, until the dough is smooth, is no longer sticky, and releases easily from the bowl or work surface.

CONTINUED ON NEXT PAGE

6. **BULK FERMENT:** Cover the dough and ferment for 2½ to 3½ hours, until doubled in volume.

7. **PREPARE THE BAKING SHEETS:** Line two flat baking sheets with parchment paper and set aside.

8. **PREPARE THE FILLING:** Place the chocolate chips in a glass or other microwave-safe bowl and microwave for 30 seconds. Add the butter and sugar and stir until smooth. Set aside.

9. **DIVIDE:** On an unfloured work surface, divide the dough into 8 pieces (about 119 grams each).

10. **SHAPE:** With a rolling pin, roll a piece of dough into a 5-by-9-inch rectangle. Brush on about ½ tablespoon (15 grams) of filling, leaving a ½-inch border along the edges. Roll the dough up from one of the long sides to the other to make a 9-inch-long rope. Use a serrated bread knife to cut the rope of dough down the center from one end to the other, leaving a ½-inch section at the end uncut. Twist the cut ends around one another three times with the inside layers facing out. Wrap the end of the twisted end around the intact end and pinch under to seal together in a twisted babka shape. Repeat with the remaining dough. Place the babka on the baking sheet 2 inches apart.

11. **PROOF:** Cover and proof for 45 minutes to 1½ hours, until about 1½ times larger in volume. Touching the dough should leave an indentation.

12. **PREHEAT:** Preheat the oven to 375°F.

13. **BAKE:** Place the first pan in the oven, reduce the heat to 350°F, and bake for 20 to 24 minutes, until the bread is golden brown. Move the finished babkas to a cooling rack. Repeat this step with the second pan.

14. **COOL:** Cool for 15 to 20 minutes on a cooling rack before serving.

TIP: Instant yeast can be omitted to create a naturally fermented bread. The fermentation and proofing process will take about 2 to 3 times longer using this method.

BRAIDED SAUSAGE-FILLED BREAKFAST BREAD

Yield: 1 (12-inch-long) filled bread

PREP TIME: 40 TO 65 MINUTES | **INACTIVE TIME:** 2 TO 3 HOURS | **BAKE TIME:** 35 TO 40 MINUTES

TOOLS NEEDED: small pot, food scale, large bowl, spoon, plastic dough scraper, skillet, spatula, slotted spoon, 2 small bowls, baking sheet, parchment paper, rolling pin, pizza cutter or large knife, pastry brush

---

For family visiting for the holidays, a breakfast potluck, or a special weekend meal, this braided sausage-filled breakfast bread is straightforward to make and looks beautiful. The hearty slices are full of flavor and so satisfying.

FOR THE DOUGH

85 grams milk (⅓ cup)

80 grams warm water, divided (⅓ cup)

2 grams instant yeast (½ teaspoon)

6 grams white cane sugar (1 teaspoon)

200 grams all-purpose flour (1⅓ cups)

50 grams whole-wheat flour (⅓ cup)

28 grams unsalted butter, at room temperature (2 tablespoons)

5 grams sea salt (¾ teaspoon)

FOR THE FILLING

½ pound ground country sausage

¼ cup shredded medium cheddar cheese

FOR THE EGG WASH

1 large egg

¼ teaspoon water

Pinch salt

1. **WARM THE MILK:** Heat the milk until it reaches a temperature of 115°F to 120°F.
2. **WEIGH THE INGREDIENTS:** Tare a mixing bowl, then combine 70 grams of warm water, 75 grams of warm milk, the instant yeast, and the sugar. Allow the sugar to dissolve, then add the all-purpose flour and whole-wheat flour.
3. **MIX:** Mix the ingredients together until a shaggy dough forms.
4. **ADD THE BUTTER AND SALT:** Fold in the butter. Add the salt to the dough, then add the remaining 10 grams of water over the salt to dissolve it. Mix to combine.
5. **KNEAD:** Turn the dough out onto a work surface and knead for 10 to 15 minutes by hand or 3 to 7 minutes with a dough hook in a stand mixer on the lowest two speeds, until the dough is smooth and elastic.

CONTINUED ON NEXT PAGE

6. **BULK FERMENT:** Cover the dough and leave in a warm place for 1½ to 2 hours, until doubled in volume.

7. **COOK THE SAUSAGE:** While the dough is fermenting, heat a skillet over medium heat. Add the country sausage and begin cooking. Use a spatula to break the meat apart so that it is crumbled into small pieces. Cook until the meat is no longer pink. Remove from the heat. Transfer the cooked sausage to a bowl with a slotted spoon. Discard any leftover grease. Set aside to cool completely.

8. **MAKE THE EGG WASH:** Beat together the egg, water, and salt; set aside.

9. **PREPARE THE BAKING SHEET:** Line a flat baking sheet with parchment paper and set aside.

10. **SHAPE:** On a lightly floured work surface, roll the dough into a rectangular shape withrounded corners, roughly 13½-by-10½ inches. Transfer to the prepared baking sheet. Use a pizza cutter to cut 1-inch-wide strips on the long sides toward the center, leaving a 3½-inch-wide uncut section down the center.

11. **FILL:** Brush the egg wash on the uncut center section of the dough. Fill the center of the bread with the sausage, keeping it off the cut strips. Sprinkle the cheese over the sausage. Wrap the first strip of dough over the filling so that it touches the other side of the dough. Wrap the first strip on the opposite side over the previous strip. Repeat this pattern until the filling is covered by the braided dough. Pinch the edges of the last strips to the bottom of the dough.

12. **PROOF:** Proof for 30 to 60 minutes.

13. **PREHEAT:** Preheat the oven to 350°F.

14. **BAKE:** Brush the outside of the braided bread with the egg wash. Bake for 35 to 40 minutes, until the bread is golden brown.

15. **COOL:** Cool for 15 to 30 minutes before slicing and serving.

PESTO WREATH BREAD

Yield: 1 large shaped bread (serves 10 to 12)

PREP TIME: 45 TO 50 MINUTES | **INACTIVE TIME:** 13 TO 20 HOURS | **BAKE TIME:** 30 TO 40 MINUTES

TOOLS NEEDED: food scale, food container, small pot, large bowl, spoon, plastic dough scraper, large cast-iron skillet (at least 10 inches in diameter) or baking sheet, parchment paper, rolling pin, serrated bread knife, small cup

Festive for the winter season with beautiful color and a savory flavor, this pesto wreath bread is a perfect appetizer for a holiday party. When you make this recipe, serving it with some warmed marinara or pizza sauce would be a delicious addition.

FOR THE STARTER
15 grams sourdough starter (1 tablespoon) or ⅛ teaspoon instant yeast

110 grams water (7½ tablespoons)

110 grams all-purpose flour (¾ cup)

FOR THE DOUGH
90 grams milk (5 tablespoons)

110 grams warm water, divided (7½ tablespoons)

5 grams white cane sugar (1 teaspoon)

3 grams instant yeast (1 teaspoon)

28 grams unsalted butter, at room temperature or melted (2 tablespoons)

200 grams starter (about 1 cup)

340 grams all-purpose flour (2¼ cups)

40 grams whole-wheat flour (¼ cup)

8 grams salt (1¼ teaspoons)

FOR THE FILLING
90 grams pesto (¼ cup)

1. **MAKE THE STARTER:** About 8 to 12 hours before mixing your dough, combine the starter or yeast, water, and flour. Mix well, cover, and leave at room temperature in a warm place to become bubbly and double in volume.

2. **WARM THE MILK:** Heat the milk until it reaches a temperature of 110°F to 120°F.

3. **WEIGH THE INGREDIENTS:** Tare a large mixing bowl, then combine 70 grams of warm milk, 100 grams of warm water, the sugar, the instant yeast, the butter, and 200 grams of starter. Once the sugar dissolves, add the all-purpose flour and whole-wheat flour.

4. **MIX:** Mix the ingredients together until a shaggy dough forms, then add the salt and the remaining 10 grams of water. Mix to combine.

5. **KNEAD:** Turn the dough out onto a work surface and knead for 10 to 15 minutes by hand or 3 to 7 minutes with a dough hook in a stand mixer on the lowest two speeds, until the dough is smooth, is no longer sticky, and releases easily from the bowl or work surface.

CONTINUED ON NEXT PAGE

6. **BULK FERMENT:** Cover the dough and ferment for 1½ to 2 hours, until doubled in volume.

7. **PREPARE THE BAKING DISH:** Line a large cast-iron skillet (or a baking sheet) with parchment.

8. **SHAPE:** On a lightly floured work surface, roll the dough into a 12-by-15-inch rectangle. Spread the pesto on top of the dough with the back of a spoon into a thin, even layer, leaving a clear ½-inch border. From the longest side, roll up the dough tightly into a long cylinder and pinch the seam closed. On top of the cylinder of dough, starting 2 inches from the end, cut lengthwise down the middle so that the inside rolled layers are exposed and there is still a connected section of dough at the top. Start at the point where the dough is connected and braid the two open halves together with the inside layers facing out. Once the entire length is braided, take the end of the braid and tuck it under the end that is uncut to create a round wreath shape. Carefully lift the wreath and place it on the center of the parchment. Place a small cup or jar in the middle of the wreath so that the center doesn't close as it proofs.

9. **PROOF:** Cover and proof in a warm place for 45 to 60 minutes, until the layers are puffy.

10. **PREHEAT:** Preheat the oven to 375°F.

11. **BAKE:** Place the skillet (or baking sheet) with the proofed wreath in the preheated oven. Bake for 30 to 40 minutes, until the bread is golden brown on the edges and baked in the center.

12. **COOL:** Let the wreath cool in the skillet (or baking sheet) for at least 20 minutes. Transfer to a plate to serve.

TIP: Instant yeast can be omitted to create a naturally fermented bread. The fermentation and proofing stages will take 2 to 3 times longer when using this method.

CHOCOLATE-SWIRLED CHALLAH

Yield: 2 medium-size loaves

PREP TIME: 40 TO 60 MINUTES | **INACTIVE TIME:** 12 TO 17 HOURS | **BAKE TIME:** 40 TO 50 MINUTES

TOOLS NEEDED: food scale, food container, large bowl, spoon, plastic dough scraper, baking sheet, parchment paper, microwave-safe bowl, spatula, rolling pin, steam pan, small bowl, pastry brush, spray bottle, cooling rack

---

The swirls of chocolate inside this bread are beautiful and make for a festive dessert or a decadent breakfast. Chocolate-swirled challah bread can be enjoyed for Hanukkah, with its rich flavors and texture.

FOR THE STARTER
30 grams sourdough starter (2 tablespoons) or ⅛ teaspoon instant yeast

15 grams white cane sugar (1 tablespoon)

50 grams water (3½ tablespoons)

100 grams all-purpose flour (⅔ cup)

FOR THE DOUGH
100 grams water (about ½ cup)

4 grams instant yeast (1 teaspoon)

150 grams starter (about ¾ cup)

500 grams bread flour (3½ cups)

2 grams ground cinnamon (½ teaspoon)

70 grams oil, such as olive oil or avocado oil (⅓ cup)

70 grams white cane sugar or honey (⅓ cup)

3 large eggs

10 grams salt (1½ teaspoons)

FOR THE FILLING
100 grams semi-sweet chocolate chips (½ cup)

30 grams oil (2 tablespoons)

75 grams white cane sugar (⅓ cup)

3 grams ground cinnamon (1 teaspoon)

FOR THE EGG WASH
1 large egg

⅛ teaspoon water

Pinch salt

Poppy seeds, for topping (optional)

1. **MAKE THE STARTER:** About 8 to 12 hours before mixing your dough, combine the starter or yeast, sugar, water, and flour in a clean container. Cover and leave at room temperature until increased in volume and bubbly.

2. **WEIGH THE INGREDIENTS:** Tare a large mixing bowl, then combine the water, instant yeast, starter, and bread flour.

3. **MIX:** Mix the ingredients together until they form a shaggy dough. Add the cinnamon, oil, sugar, eggs, and salt. Continue mixing.

CONTINUED ON NEXT PAGE

4. **KNEAD:** Turn the dough out onto a work surface and knead for 10 to 15 minutes by hand or 4 to 8 minutes with a dough hook in a stand mixer on the lowest two speeds, until the dough is smooth, is no longer sticky, and releases easily from the bowl or work surface.

5. **BULK FERMENT:** Cover the dough and ferment for 2 to 3 hours, until doubled in volume.

6. **PREPARE THE BAKING SHEET:** Line a baking sheet with parchment paper and set aside.

7. **DIVIDE:** Divide the dough into four equal pieces for two medium loaves.

8. **PREPARE THE FILLING:** Place the chocolate chips in a microwave-safe bowl and microwave for about 30 seconds. Stir the chocolate to ensure it's fully melted, then add the oil, sugar, and cinnamon and stir until the mixture reaches a spreadable consistency. If the filling is too runny, add an additional 10 grams of sugar.

9. **FILL THE DOUGH:** On a lightly floured work surface, roll a piece of dough into a 7-by-11-inch rectangle. Spread one-quarter of the filling onto the dough, leaving a 1-inch border around the outside. From one of the long sides of the dough, begin rolling the dough onto itself until it is a long rope shape. Pinch the seam firmly together to seal. Repeat with the remaining pieces of dough.

10. **BRAID:** Gently loosen and elongate two of the ropes of dough by holding the ends and shaking until the rope stretches to 12 to 13 inches long. To braid the sections of dough, cross the two ropes of dough over each other into an "X" shape. Take the upper two sections of the ropes of dough and pull down toward the bottom so that all four edges are pointed downward. From left to right, think of the pieces of dough as 1, 2, 3, and 4. Bring 1 over 2, 3 over 4, 4 over 1, 2 over 4, 1 over 3, and 3 over 2, then tuck all the strands under and firmly pinch the tips of the ropes to the bottom of the shape to hold the braid in place. The filled ropes are thicker than traditional challah plaits, so they may take more effort to braid. If you can do a few more knots than described, feel free to add them. Repeat this step with the remaining two ropes.

11. **PROOF:** Place the loaves on the prepared baking sheet. Cover and proof for 45 to 90 minutes, until about doubled in size.

12. **PREHEAT:** Near the end of the proofing period, preheat the oven to 375°F and place a steam pan filled with water on the lowest rack.

13. **MAKE THE EGG WASH:** Beat together the egg, water, and salt; brush the egg wash over the tops of the loaves. Sprinkle poppy seeds over the egg wash (if using).

14. **BAKE:** Place the pan of challah in the oven. Reduce the heat to 350°F and bake for 25 minutes. Remove the steam pan and continue baking for 15 to 25 minutes longer, until the loaves are a shiny golden brown, paying attention to the sections of dough between the braids for doneness.

15. **COOL:** Transfer the loaves to a cooling rack and cool for 1 hour.

TIP: Instant yeast can be omitted to create a naturally fermented bread. The fermentation and proofing processes will take 2 to 3 times longer using this method.

ST. LUCIA BUNS

Yield: 20 buns

PREP TIME: 55 TO 60 MINUTES | **INACTIVE TIME:** 13 TO 18 HOURS | **BAKE TIME:** 14 TO 16 MINUTES

TOOLS NEEDED: food scale, food container, small pot, large bowl, spoon, plastic dough scraper, 2 baking sheets, parchment paper, small bowl, pastry brush

In Sweden and other Scandinavian countries, the beginning of the Christmas season is always marked by celebrating St. Lucia. These golden-hued sweet buns are traditionally enjoyed with friends and family to spread light in the darkest part of winter.

FOR THE STARTER

30 grams sourdough starter (2 tablespoons) or ⅛ teaspoon instant yeast

15 grams white cane sugar (1 tablespoon)

50 grams water (3½ tablespoons)

100 grams all-purpose flour (⅔ cup)

FOR THE DOUGH

160 grams milk (5 tablespoons)

1 gram saffron threads (about 4 pinches)

60 grams warm water, divided (¼ cup)

150 grams starter (about ¾ cup)

80 grams white cane sugar (¼ cup plus 2½ tablespoons)

4 grams instant yeast (1 teaspoon)

520 grams all-purpose flour (3½ cups)

1 large egg

2 large egg yolks

8 grams sea salt (1¼ teaspoons)

113 grams unsalted butter, melted (8 tablespoons)

FOR THE EGG WASH

1 large egg

¼ teaspoon water

Pearl sugar, for topping (optional)

1. **MAKE THE STARTER:** About 8 to 12 hours before mixing your dough, combine the starter or yeast, sugar, water, and flour in a clean container. Cover and leave at room temperature. It will increase in volume and become bubbly.

2. **WARM THE MILK:** Heat the milk and saffron threads in a small pot until it reaches a temperature of 130°F to 140°F. Let the milk stand for 20 minutes to deepen the color.

3. **WEIGH THE INGREDIENTS:** Tare a large mixing bowl, then combine 140 grams of warm saffron milk, 50 grams of warm water, 150 grams of starter, the sugar, and the instant yeast. Allow the sugar to dissolve, then add the flour.

4. **MIX:** Mix the ingredients together until a shaggy dough forms, then add the egg, egg yolks, remaining 10 grams of water, and salt. Mix into the dough until the ingredients are combined.

5. **ADD THE BUTTER:** Add the warm melted butter to the dough. Mix to combine.

6. **KNEAD:** Turn the dough out onto a work surface and knead for 10 to 15 minutes by hand or 3 to 8 minutes with a dough hook in a stand mixer on the lowest two speeds, until the dough is smooth, is no longer sticky, and releases easily from the bowl or work surface.

7. **BULK FERMENT:** Cover the dough and ferment for 3½ to 4½ hours, until doubled in volume.

8. **PREPARE THE BAKING SHEETS:** Line two flat baking sheets with parchment paper and set aside.

9. **DIVIDE:** Divide the dough into 20 equal pieces (about 56 grams each).

10. **SHAPE:** Roll a piece of dough under your hands into a 10- to 11-inch rope with tapered ends. Curve the rope into an S shape, then curl the ends in toward the middle to create two spirals. The bun should be about 3½ inches long. Place the bun on one of the prepared baking sheets. Repeat with the remaining pieces of dough, spacing the buns about 2 inches apart.

11. **PROOF:** Cover and proof for 45 to 75 minutes. The dough should expand and leave an indentation when touched.

12. **PREHEAT:** Preheat the oven to 375°F.

13. **MAKE THE EGG WASH:** Beat together the egg and water. Brush the egg wash all over the buns. Sprinkle the pearl sugar (if using) over the egg wash.

14. **BAKE:** Bake for 14 to 16 minutes, until the buns are golden brown.

15. **COOL:** Allow the buns to cool for 10 to 15 minutes before serving.

TIP: Instant yeast can be omitted to create a naturally fermented bread. The fermentation and proofing will take 2 to 3 times longer using this method.

STEAMED ROSE-SHAPED BUNS

Yield: 16 rose buns

PREP TIME: 70 TO 90 MINUTES | **INACTIVE TIME:** 3 TO 4 HOURS | **BAKE TIME:** 16 TO 18 MINUTES

TOOLS NEEDED: pot, food scale, strainer, large bowl, spoon, plastic dough scraper, 2-tier bamboo steamer, parchment paper for steaming, rolling pin, large wok or large pot with steaming adapter

Sweetly flavored and adorably shaped, these steamed rose-shaped buns are the perfect treat for Valentine's Day, birthday parties, or Lunar New Year. The shaping method is very specific, but the results are so satisfying and beautiful.

FOR THE RED DYED WATER
2 cups water

500 grams raw red beets, root and stem removed (3 medium-size beets)

FOR THE DOUGH
200 grams red dyed water (¾ cup plus 2 tablespoons)

50 grams white cane sugar (¼ cup)

4 grams instant yeast (1 teaspoon)

400 grams all-purpose flour (2⅔ cups)

8 grams dried beet powder (1 teaspoon)

12 grams lard, at room temperature (1 tablespoon)

4 grams vanilla extract (1 teaspoon) or 4 grams rose extract (½ teaspoon)

5 grams baking powder (1 teaspoon)

2 grams salt (¼ teaspoon)

1. **MAKE THE DYED WATER:** This step can be done up to a week ahead of time. Bring the water to boil in a medium-size pot. Add the beets, cover, and reduce the heat to simmer for 15 minutes. Turn off the heat, leaving the lid on, and let the mixture sit for 30 to 60 minutes, until the water cools to room temperature. Strain the liquid and set aside or store in a sealed container in the refrigerator.

2. **WEIGH THE INGREDIENTS:** Tare a mixing bowl, then combine 200 grams of dyed water, the sugar, and the instant yeast. Allow the sugar to dissolve. Add the flour and beet powder, then stir the mixture 3 or 4 times to incorporate. Add the lard, vanilla or rose extract, and baking powder.

3. **MIX:** Mix the ingredients together until a shaggy dough forms, then add the salt. Mix to combine.

4. **KNEAD:** Turn the dough out onto a work surface and knead for 10 to 15 minutes by hand or 4 to 8 minutes with a dough hook in a stand mixer on the lowest two speeds, until the dough is smooth, is no longer sticky, and releases easily from the bowl or work surface. I recommend kneading on a non-staining work surface because the beet will dye any wood or porous surfaces.

5. **BULK FERMENT:** Cover the dough and ferment for 1½ to 2 hours, until doubled in volume.

6. **PREPARE THE STEAMER:** Line two bamboo steam trays with round sheets of parchment made for bamboo steamers.

7. **DIVIDE:** Divide the dough into 48 equal pieces (12 to 14 grams each). Roll each piece into a ball and cover with plastic wrap or a cloth to keep the dough from drying out.

8. **SHAPE:** Take 6 pieces of dough. With a rolling pin, roll a piece into a 3½-inch round disc. Roll a second piece in the same way. Place the second disc over half of the first disc so that they are overlapped. Repeat this process with the other 4 pieces of dough so that each successive disc overlaps half of the previous disc and there is a line of overlapped discs about 24½ inches long. Start at the first disc you rolled (the bottom-most layer) and begin rolling the dough up tightly until all the discs are rolled into each other. Use the sharp edge of the dough scraper or a knife to cut the tube of rolled dough in half. Turn each half onto the cut side and you will see the layers of dough have created your rose shape. Place the roses cut-side down into the prepared steamer trays. Repeat with the rest of the pieces of dough until you have 16 roses, 8 in each steamer tray, spaced evenly apart.

9. **PROOF:** Stack the bamboo steam trays and place the cover on top. Proof in a warm place for 30 to 45 minutes, until at least 1½ times larger.

10. **BOIL THE WATER:** Place a large wok filled with 2 to 3 inches of water over high heat. Bring to a boil.

11. **STEAM AND SERVE:** Place the stacked bamboo steamer into the wok, reduce the heat to medium, and steam for 16 to 18 minutes. After 12 minutes, rotate the steamer tray layers for even steaming. The bottom of the steamer should stay submerged in water, but the water should not reach higher than ¼ inch up the side. After the cooking time, turn off the heat and let the buns sit covered for an additional 5 to 10 minutes. Serve fresh.

TIP: You may substitute diluted red food dye for the beet-dyed water and beet powder; just add 1 more tablespoon of flour to your dough to account for the change in texture. Or use undyed water for off-white roses.

MUSHROOM BAOZI

Yield: 12 baozi

PREP TIME: 40 TO 55 MINUTES | **INACTIVE TIME:** 3 TO 4 HOURS | **BAKE TIME:** 16 TO 18 MINUTES

TOOLS NEEDED: food scale, large bowl, spoon, plastic dough scraper, knife, pot or skillet, 2-tier bamboo steamer, parchment paper for steaming, rolling pin, large wok or large pot with steaming adapter

These mushroom baozi are an excellent vegetarian way to celebrate the Lunar New Year. The buns have a cakey texture when you bite into them. Kneading the dough adequately is the key to getting a smooth, round shape to your baozi.

FOR THE DOUGH

200 grams warm water
(¾ cup plus 2 tablespoons)

5 grams white cane
sugar (1 teaspoon)

6 grams instant yeast
(1½ teaspoons)

400 grams all-purpose
flour (2⅔ cups)

40 grams arrowroot
powder (⅓ cup)

20 grams oil, such as avocado
oil, olive oil, or vegetable oil
(1 tablespoon plus 1 teaspoon)

4 grams baking powder
(½ teaspoon)

4 grams salt (½ teaspoon)

FOR THE FILLING

300 grams mushrooms,
white or baby bella (about
24 mushrooms)

1 tablespoon oil

4 garlic cloves, minced

2 teaspoons honey

2 tablespoons soy sauce

2 tablespoons oyster sauce

½ teaspoon fresh grated ginger

2 scallions, finely sliced

1. **WEIGH THE INGREDIENTS:** Tare a mixing bowl, then combine the warm water, sugar, and instant yeast. Allow the sugar to dissolve, then add the flour, arrowroot powder, oil, and baking powder.

2. **MIX:** Mix the ingredients together until a shaggy dough forms, then add the salt. Mix to combine.

3. **KNEAD:** Turn the dough out onto a work surface and knead for 10 to 15 minutes by hand or 5 to 8 minutes with a dough hook in a stand mixer on the lowest two speeds,

until the dough is very smooth and no longer has a rough texture.

4. **BULK FERMENT:** Cover the dough and ferment for 1½ to 2 hours, until doubled in volume.

5. **MAKE THE FILLING:** While the dough is rising, cut the mushrooms into ¼-inch pieces. In a small pot or large skillet over medium heat, warm the oil, then add the garlic and mushrooms. Sauté until softened. Add the honey, soy sauce, oyster sauce, and ginger. Continue to cook, stirring frequently, until

the mixture is fragrant and the mushrooms are cooked. Remove from the heat. Stir in the scallions and set aside to cool.

6. **PREPARE THE STEAMER:** Line two bamboo steam trays with round sheets of parchment made for bamboo steamers.

7. **DIVIDE:** Divide the dough into 12 equal pieces (about 27 grams each) and roll each piece into a ball. Cover the balls of dough with a cloth to keep them from drying out.

8. **SHAPE:** Make sure the filling is completely cooled before beginning to shape the buns. With a rolling pin, roll a piece of dough into a thin circle, about 4¾ inches wide. Make sure that the edges of the circle are slightly thinner than the middle. Place 1½ to 2 tablespoons of the filling in the very center of the circle, reserving a 1-inch border. Gather an edge of the dough into the center, over the filling. Make a ¼-inch crimp in the dough at the top, then gather another section of dough and make another ¼-inch crimp next to the first one. Pinch to make sure the crimps do not come undone. Continue to crimp around the entire filling

until there's only a small ¼- to ½-inch opening at the top. Place the shaped baozi in the prepared steamer tray. Repeat with the rest of the pieces of dough and filling. There should be 6 shaped baozi in each tray, spaced evenly apart.

9. **PROOF:** Stack the bamboo steam trays and place the cover on top. Let the baozi rest for 20 minutes.

10. **HEAT THE WOK:** Place a large wok filled with 2 to 3 inches of water on the stovetop. Do not preheat before placing the steamer on, but place the steamer in the wok with the cold water. Turn up the heat to bring the water to a boil. As soon as the water is boiling, reduce the heat to medium-low.

11. **STEAM AND SERVE:** Steam for 16 to 18 minutes. After 13 minutes, rotate the steamer tray layers for even steaming. The bottom of the steamer should stay submerged in water, but the water should reach no higher than ¼ inch up the side. After 15 minutes, turn off the heat and let the buns sit covered for an additional 5 to 10 minutes. Serve fresh.

NORWEGIAN-INSPIRED LEFSE

Yield: 36 lefse

PREP TIME: 45 TO 70 MINUTES | **INACTIVE TIME:** 40 TO 80 MINUTES
BAKE TIME: 1 TO 2 MINUTES PER LEFSE

TOOLS NEEDED: large pot, food scale, colander, potato ricer, large bowl, spoon, lefse-making kit or a thick linen cloth or tablecloth and 2 flat wood flipping tools or spatulas and rolling pin, large skillet or pan, large plate, kitchen towel

Lefse making is a holiday tradition in many Scandinavian households and is often a team effort. These delicate potato crepes are delicious and bring everyone together. If it's your first time making lefse, be sure to read through the tips and keep your sense of humor because getting the first ones shaped and cooked is always the most difficult part.

6 large russet potatoes, peeled

120 grams unsalted butter, plus more for serving
(½ cup plus ½ tablespoon)

120 grams whole milk
(½ cup plus ½ tablespoon)

7 grams white cane sugar
(1¼ teaspoons)

7 grams salt (1¼ teaspoons)

3 grams ground cardamom
(1 teaspoon) (optional)

240 grams all-purpose flour
(1½ cups plus 2 tablespoons)

Cinnamon sugar, for serving

1. **BOIL THE POTATOES:** Bring a large (5-quart or larger) pot of water to a boil. Once the water is boiling, add the potatoes and boil for 25 to 30 minutes, until fork-tender.

2. **RICE THE POTATOES:** Once the potatoes are fork-tender, strain them in a colander and run cool water over them. Press your cooked potatoes through a ricer into a large mixing bowl until you have 1,200 grams, or about 9 cups, of riced potatoes.

3. **WEIGH THE INGREDIENTS:** Tare the bowl, then combine the butter, whole milk, sugar, salt, and cardamom (if using). Stir everything together and set aside to cool.

4. **PREPARE THE COOKING AREA:** Lefse are very delicate due to the very high percentage of potato used in the dough. To prepare your cooking area without a kit, lay out a large cloth towel or tablecloth (cotton linen works best, whereas terry cloth will be problematic) on a work surface close to your stovetop. Apply a generous coating of flour to the cloth and rub it into the fabric. Coat a rolling pin in flour. (If you have a new, unused sock, you can cut off the toe and pull the sock onto a standard rolling pin and coat the sock in flour instead.) Get two spatulas ready to transfer the shaped lefse. (Flat wood spatulas work well.) Preheat a large skillet over medium-high heat. Finally, get a large plate ready with a kitchen towel to cover the cooked lefse.

5. **ADD THE FLOUR:** Once the potato mixture has cooled to room temperature, tare the bowl and add the flour. Mix everything together until it forms a dough that holds together when rolled into a ball.

6. **DIVIDE:** Begin tearing off 36 pieces of the dough and rolling them into golf ball–size pieces (about 47 grams each). You can put the balls back into the same mixing bowl.

7. **CHILL THE DOUGH:** Place the dough balls in the refrigerator and let them chill for at least 20 minutes.

8. **SHAPE:** Apply a fresh coating of flour to the linen on your work surface and to the rolling pin. Place a ball of lefse dough in the center of your space. Begin rolling it out, reapplying a thin coating of flour to the rolling pin every one or two rolls if you are not using one from a lefse-making kit or the DIY sock-covered rolling pin. If the rolling pin starts sticking to the lefse, the dough will tear. Roll the dough until it is a 7- to 8-inch-wide circle that is thin enough to read a newspaper through (thinner than a tortilla).

9. **COOK:** Once the dough is rolled and the skillet is preheated, use the two spatulas to gently lift the dough off the cloth. Lay it on the hot skillet and cook for 30 to 45 seconds, until it starts to bubble and brown spots appear on the bottom. Flip and cook for another 30 seconds or until brown spots appear. Remove from the skillet, place on the plate, and cover with the kitchen towel.

10. **REPEAT:** Repeat steps 8 and 9 with another ball of dough. Unless you are making lefse with an assembly line of friends or family members, don't roll out the next lefse while one is still cooking, due to how quickly these cook.

11. **SERVE:** Spread butter on the lefse, followed by a sprinkling of cinnamon sugar. Fold in half, roll up, and enjoy!

TIPS: If you are having trouble forming a dough that holds together, add 1 tablespoon of flour and mix again. If you are having difficulty rolling out the lefse, let the dough chill in the refrigerator longer. You don't want to overflour this dough, but the rolling pin and the linen must be sufficiently floured to keep the lefse from sticking and tearing.

Lefse can be covered in plastic wrap and stored at room temperature or in the refrigerator for 5 to 7 days, or they can be wrapped in plastic wrap and aluminum foil and frozen for up to 1 month.

STOLLEN

Yield: 2 loaves

PREP TIME: 2 HOURS | **INACTIVE TIME:** 12 TO 17 HOURS | **BAKE TIME:** 30 TO 40 MINUTES

TOOLS NEEDED: sharp knife, small pot, fine-mesh strainer, slotted spoon, cooling rack, food scale, 2 large bowls, spoon, food processor, food container, zester, plastic dough scraper, baking sheet, parchment paper, toothpick

With a bread this special, there aren't a lot of shortcuts. But because it's only made once each year, traditionally at Christmas, it's worth taking the time to make this extravagantly rich and flavored bread the right way.

FOR THE CANDIED PEELS

1 orange

1 lemon

1 cup water

2 cups white cane sugar

FOR THE RUM-SOAKED FRUIT AND NUTS

90 grams candied peels (⅔ cup)

30 grams almonds, chopped (¼ cup)

50 grams raisins (⅓ cup)

50 grams golden raisins (⅓ cup)

150 grams rum (⅔ cup)

FOR THE MARZIPAN

1 cup very finely ground almond flour or meal

1 cup powdered sugar

1½ teaspoons pure almond extract

¾ teaspoon rose water (optional)

1 large egg white

FOR THE STARTER

42 grams sourdough starter (3 tablespoons) or ⅛ teaspoon instant yeast

70 grams water (4¾ tablespoons)

20 grams white cane sugar (1 tablespoon plus 1 teaspoon)

140 grams all-purpose flour (1 cup minus 1 tablespoon)

FOR THE DOUGH

240 grams milk (1 cup)

50 grams white cane sugar (¼ cup)

3 grams instant yeast (½ teaspoon)

190 grams starter (about 1½ cups)

450 grams bread flour (2⅔ cups)

50 grams whole-wheat flour (⅓ cup)

2 grams ground cloves (½ teaspoon)

1 gram ground cardamom (¼ teaspoon)

2 grams ground cinnamon (½ teaspoon)

1 large egg

2 large egg yolks

8 grams vanilla extract (2 teaspoons)

Zest of 1 lemon

7 grams salt (1 teaspoon)

120 grams unsalted butter, at room temperature (½ cup plus ½ tablespoon)

FOR THE TOPPING

½ cup unsalted butter, melted

¼ to ½ cup powdered sugar

1. **MAKE THE CANDIED PEELS:** This step can be done up to two weeks in advance or when mixing the starter. Carefully cut the peel off the lemon and orange. Trim off any fruit,

leaving only the peel with some of the pith. Slice into thin strips, then cut into ¼- to ½-inch pieces. Bring a pot of water to a boil. Boil the peels for 15 minutes, then strain and rinse them. Empty the water from the pot and repeat the boiling process to remove any residual bitter flavors. Add the water and 1 cup of white cane sugar to the pot and bring to a boil. When all the sugar has dissolved, add the peels and reduce the heat to a simmer. Let the peels cook for 15 to 20 minutes, until the liquid is syrupy and the peels are translucent. Carefully remove the peels from the pot with a slotted spoon and place on a cooling rack. Once cooled, toss the peels with the remaining 1 cup of sugar to coat. Store in a jar for up to two weeks.

2. **MAKE THE RUM-SOAKED FRUIT AND NUT MIXTURE:** Mix together the candied peels, almonds, raisins, golden raisins, and rum. Mix the ingredients together so that they are all covered by the rum. Let soak for at least 10 hours. You can start soaking these before you make your starter to streamline the process.

3. **MAKE THE MARZIPAN:** This step can be done up to 1 month in advance. In a food processor, blend the almond flour and powdered sugar until completely combined without any lumps. Add the almond extract and rose water (if using). Pulse together, then add the egg white. Process until a thick dough is formed. Knead and shape into a log. Wrap in plastic wrap and refrigerate.

4. **MAKE THE STARTER:** About 10 to 12 hours before mixing your dough, combine the starter or yeast, water, sugar, and flour in a bowl or container. Cover and leave at room temperature until doubled.

5. **WARM THE MILK:** Heat the milk until it reaches a temperature of 115°F to 120°F.

6. **WEIGH THE INGREDIENTS:** Tare a large mixing bowl, then combine 230 grams of warm milk, the sugar, the instant yeast, and 190 grams of starter. Add the bread flour, whole-wheat flour, cloves, cardamom, and cinnamon.

7. **MIX:** Mix the ingredients together until a shaggy dough forms, then add the egg, egg yolks, vanilla, lemon zest, and salt. Mix to combine.

8. **ADD THE BUTTER:** Add the butter and knead into the dough.

9. **KNEAD:** Turn the dough out onto a work surface and knead for 10 to 15 minutes by hand or 4 to 8 minutes with a dough hook in a stand mixer on the lowest two speeds, until the dough is smooth, is no longer sticky, and releases easily from the bowl or work surface.

10. **ADD THE RUM-SOAKED FRUIT AND NUTS:** Strain the rum-soaked fruit and nut mixture in a fine-mesh strainer. Shake off any excess rum. Place the soaked fruit and nuts in the center of the dough. Fold to incorporate the fruit and nuts throughout the dough.

11. **BULK FERMENT:** Cover the dough and ferment for 1½ to 3 hours, until doubled in volume.

CONTINUED ON NEXT PAGE

12. **PREPARE THE BAKING SHEET:** Line a flat baking sheet with parchment paper and set aside.

13. **PREPARE THE MARZIPAN:** Divide the marzipan into two pieces. Roll each piece into a 7-inch-long cylinder. Set aside.

14. **DIVIDE:** Place the dough on a lightly floured work surface. Divide in half.

15. **SHAPE:** Take one half of the dough and pat it out until it is a large oval shape that is about 1 inch thick, 8 inches long, and 5 to 6 inches wide. Place a cylinder of marzipan in the center of the dough, then take a long edge of the dough and fold it over the marzipan and seal 1 inch away from the other side to form the traditional ledge on the edge. Gently press the side of your hand along this ledge to seal. The marzipan should be completely covered. Repeat this process with the other half of the dough.

16. **PROOF:** Cover and proof for 45 to 75 minutes, until about 1½ times larger in volume. Touching the dough should leave an indentation.

17. **PREHEAT:** Preheat the oven to 375°F.

18. **BAKE:** Place the pan in the oven, reduce the temperature to 350°F, and bake for 30 to 40 minutes. The bread should have a golden-brown top, and the internal temperature of the loaves should be 190°F.

19. **COOL:** Allow the loaves to rest for 15 to 20 minutes.

20. **PREPARE THE TOPPING:** Poke holes all over the stollen with a toothpick. Pour the melted butter slowly over the top, allowing it to seep in. Generously dust with powdered sugar. Cool for an additional 10 to 20 minutes, until no longer steaming, before cutting.

21. **SERVE:** Cut the stollen into slices to serve right away or wrap the loaves after they've cooled. Wait at least 12 hours for the flavors to deepen for an even more decadent treat.

PANETTONE

Yield: 2 large panettone

PREP TIME: 2 TO 2½ HOURS | **INACTIVE TIME:** 22 TO 41 HOURS | **BAKE TIME:** 30 TO 35 MINUTES

TOOLS NEEDED: food scale, food container, knife, pot, slotted spoon, cooling rack, large bowl, spoon, 2 storage containers with at least 8-quart capacity, small bowl, fine-mesh strainer, electric stand mixer (recommended), zester, plastic dough scraper, 4 skewers, 2 large paper panettone paper molds (5½- to 6¾-inch diameter), bowl, whisk

Panettone is an iconic Christmas bread that comes to us from Milan, Italy. It is time-consuming to make, but the flavor and texture in a good panettone is a special pleasure of Christmastime baking.

FOR THE CANDIED PEELS

1 orange

1 lemon

1 cup water

2 cups white cane sugar

FOR THE RUM-SOAKED RAISINS

50 grams raisins (⅓ cup)

50 grams golden raisins (⅓ cup)

30 grams rum (2 tablespoons)

30 grams hot water (2 tablespoons)

FOR THE STARTER

30 grams sourdough starter (2 tablespoons)

30 grams white cane sugar (2 tablespoons)

100 grams water (6 tablespoons plus 2 teaspoons)

200 grams bread flour (1⅓ cups)

FOR THE FIRST DOUGH

120 grams room-temperature water (½ cup plus 2 tablespoons)

200 grams starter (about 1 cup)

4 grams instant yeast (1 teaspoon)

300 grams bread flour (2 cups)

4 large egg yolks (about 65 grams)

40 grams white cane sugar (2 tablespoons plus 2 teaspoons)

84 grams unsalted butter, at room temperature (6 tablespoons)

FOR THE FINAL DOUGH

80 grams bread flour (½ cup plus ½ tablespoon)

50 grams room-temperature water (3 tablespoons plus 1 teaspoon)

6 grams salt (scant teaspoon)

2 large egg yolks

20 grams white cane sugar (1 tablespoon plus 1 teaspoon)

Zest of 1 orange

1 vanilla bean pod (optional)

84 grams unsalted butter, at room temperature, plus more for greasing containers (6 tablespoons)

60 grams candied peels (¼ cup)

FOR THE GLAZE

2 large egg whites

55 grams powdered sugar (⅓ cup)

10 grams all-purpose flour (1 tablespoon)

¼ teaspoon vanilla extract

Swedish pearl sugar, for topping (optional)

Sliced almonds, for topping (optional)

CONTINUED ON NEXT PAGE

1. **MAKE THE STARTER:** Make sure your sourdough starter is active and has been refreshed at least once in the last 8 to 12 hours. In a clean container, measure in the starter, sugar, water, and bread flour. Mix by hand to make sure all the water is absorbed. Leave at room temperature to become active for 8 to 10 hours, until doubled in size, thick, and puffy.

2. **MAKE THE CANDIED FRUIT PEELS:** Follow the directions on step 1 of the Stollen recipe on page 132 to make the candied fruit peels. This step can be done up to a week in advance.

3. **WEIGH THE INGREDIENTS FOR THE FIRST DOUGH:** Tare your mixing bowl, then combine the room-temperature water, 200 grams of starter prepared in step 1, and the instant yeast. Once the yeast dissolves, add the bread flour.

4. **MIX:** Using the dough hook, mix everything together in a stand mixer until the dough is coming together and the flour has absorbed all the water.

5. **ADD THE EGG YOLKS:** Add half of the egg yolks and mix until they are completely incorporated, then mix in the rest of the egg yolks. Continue mixing until the dough becomes smooth and elastic.

6. **ADD THE SUGAR:** Add 10 grams of sugar and fold in until incorporated, about 1 minute. Add the rest of the sugar 10 grams at a time, mixing in after each addition.

7. **ADD THE BUTTER:** Once the dough appears smooth, add the butter 1 tablespoon at a time, folding the dough until the butter is completely incorporated after each addition.

8. **FIRST RISE:** Move the dough to a large container. Cover and leave at room temperature for 6 to 12 hours, until tripled in volume. (A colder room will make the rising take longer; a warmer room will take less time.)

9. **MAKE THE RUM-SOAKED RAISINS:** While the dough is rising, mix the raisins, golden raisins, rum, and hot water together in a small bowl. The raisins should soak in the rum for at least 8 hours.

10. **DRAIN THE RUM-SOAKED RAISINS:** Pour the rum-soaked raisins into a fine-mesh strainer and allow the water and rum to drain. Set aside.

11. **MAKE THE FINAL DOUGH:** Place the dough back in the mixing bowl of the stand mixer. Tare the bowl, then add the bread flour and water. Begin mixing with a dough hook on low speed for 1 to 2 minutes. Add the salt and egg yolks. Continue mixing on low until the dough is becoming smooth and the flour has been absorbed. Slowly add the sugar 10 grams at a time, then add the orange zest. Scrape the vanilla out of the inside of the bean (if using) and add it to the bowl.

12. **ADD THE BUTTER:** The dough should be strong and elastic. Check the strength by

pulling a small section and seeing if light shows through it when stretched. If it is strong enough, add the butter 1 tablespoon at a time, mixing for 30 to 60 seconds afterward to incorporate.

13. **ADD THE FRUIT:** Fold in the drained raisins and candied fruit peels until dispersed throughout. Grease a new container (with at least an 8-quart capacity) with unsalted butter for the dough's second rise. Move the dough to the prepped container to continue rising.

14. **SECOND RISE:** Cover the dough and leave at room temperature for 1 hour. After 30 minutes, stretch and fold the dough, then cover it back up.

15. **PRE-SHAPE:** Grease about a 2-square-foot area of your work surface with unsalted butter. Use the sharp edge of a plastic dough scraper to divide the dough in half. Push the edges of each piece under to form a loose round shape. Let the dough rest for 20 minutes.

16. **PREPARE THE PANETTONE MOLDS:** Take the 4 skewers and poke through the panettone molds 1 inch from the bottom in parallel lines. These will be used to suspend the panettone upside down as they cool.

17. **SHAPE:** Grease your hands to keep them from sticking to the dough. Use the edge of a dough scraper to rotate the dough in a circular motion until it forms a tight ball, then slide the scraper under the ball of dough and lift with your opposite hand to guide it into the prepared panettone mold. Repeat with the other section of dough.

18. **PROOF:** Cover each mold with a piece of plastic wrap and proof at room temperature for 3 to 6 hours, until the top of the dough is nearly at the top of the mold and the edges of the dough are about 1 inch away from the rim.

19. **PREHEAT:** Preheat the oven to 350°F.

20. **PREPARE THE COOLING AREA:** Panettone will collapse if they are not hung upside down after baking. Prepare an area where they can hang upside down using sturdy stools, storage bins, etc.

21. **GLAZE:** Whisk the egg whites, powdered sugar, flour, and vanilla together until frothy. Brush the glaze on the tops of the panettone. Sprinkle on the pearl sugar and/or almonds (if using).

22. **BAKE:** Place the glazed panettone on the center oven rack. Bake for 30 to 35 minutes. Check after 25 minutes. If the top is becoming too dark, turn the oven temperature down to 325°F. The tops of the panettone should be a dark, rich brown color and should have a dome rising over the rim of the mold.

23. **COOL:** As soon as the panettone come out of the oven, turn them upside down to hang in your prepared area. They must cool upside down to set for at least 4 hours, or overnight if possible. Cut straight through the paper molds and peel them off, then cut the panettone into slices and serve.

Mini Pain d'Épi, page 162

Chapter Six

SPECIAL OCCASIONS

Gather your family, celebrate your friends, and break bread together all year round for birthdays, weekend visits, and other special occasions.

BEER BREAD

Yield: 1 loaf

PREP TIME: 20 TO 30 MINUTES | **INACTIVE TIME:** 20 TO 30 MINUTES | **BAKE TIME:** 40 TO 45 MINUTES

TOOLS NEEDED: food scale, large mixing bowl, spoon, loaf pan, parchment paper, spatula

Beer bread is so easy to make and tastes delicious. It can be put together quickly for a dinner with friends, game night, potluck, or any other special occasion. It has a texture similar to corn bread, but the beer gives it a sweet, complex flavor.

380 grams all-purpose flour (2⅔ cups)

70 grams whole-wheat flour (½ cup)

15 grams baking powder (1 tablespoon)

4 grams salt (½ teaspoon)

30 grams white cane sugar (2 tablespoons)

1 (12-ounce) bottle or can of beer

28 grams unsalted butter, melted (2 tablespoons)

1. **PREHEAT:** Preheat the oven to 375°F.
2. **WEIGH THE INGREDIENTS:** Tare a large mixing bowl, then combine the all-purpose flour, whole-wheat flour, baking powder, salt, and sugar.
3. **ADD THE BEER:** Stir the dry ingredients together, then make a well in the center. Pour in the beer.
4. **MIX:** Mix the beer into the dry mixture until it is almost completely incorporated. Add in the melted butter. Stir until it becomes a thick batter and there are no dry ingredients left, but be careful not to overmix.
5. **PREPARE THE LOAF PAN:** Line a loaf pan with parchment paper and set aside. (See step 6 of Zucchini Spice Quick Bread on page 44.)
6. **FILL THE LOAF PAN:** Using a spatula, add the batter to the loaf pan.
7. **BAKE:** Place the pan in the oven and bake for 40 to 45 minutes, until a toothpick or knife inserted into the center comes out clean.
8. **COOL AND SERVE:** Allow to cool for 20 to 30 minutes, then slice and serve.

EASY TACO NIGHT TORTILLAS

Yield: 24 tortillas

PREP TIME: 30 TO 45 MINUTES | **BAKE TIME:** 1 MINUTE PER TORTILLA

TOOLS NEEDED: food container, paper towel, food scale, large bowl,
spoon, plastic dough scraper, rolling pin, large skillet or pan

*Taco night is a tradition in many households. Tacos can be very simple or topped
with a wide variety of ingredients, but it's essential to always start with a good
tortilla. This recipe is essentially foolproof and creates delicious flour tortillas.*

300 grams all-purpose
flour (2 cups)

12 grams salt (1½ teaspoons)

45 grams oil, such as
coconut oil, avocado oil,
or lard (3 tablespoons)

180 grams very warm water
(110°F to 130°F) (¾ cup)

1. **PREPARE A CONTAINER:** Use a food container
   with a lid, like a glass food storage
   container or a large bowl or pie dish with
   a plate over it. Line the bottom with a
   paper towel.

2. **WEIGH THE INGREDIENTS:** Making sure to
   tare after each addition, combine the flour
   and salt in a mixing bowl. Stir together. Add
   the oil and water.

3. **KNEAD:** Turn the dough out onto a work
   surface and knead for 8 to 12 minutes by
   hand or 3 to 7 minutes with a dough hook
   in a stand mixer on the lowest two speeds,
   until the dough is smooth, is no longer
   sticky, and releases easily from the bowl or
   work surface.

4. **DIVIDE:** Divide the dough into 24 equal
   pieces (about 22 grams each) and roll each
   piece into a ball. Cover with plastic wrap or
   a cloth.

5. **HEAT THE SKILLET:** Heat a large pan or skillet
   over medium-high heat.

6. **SHAPE:** Roll a ball of dough with a rolling
   pin until it's about 5 inches wide and very
   thin. You should be able to read through it if
   you lay it on a page of a book.

7. **COOK:** Place a tortilla in the skillet and cook
   for 30 seconds or until the tortilla begins
   to bubble. Flip and cook on the other side
   for 30 seconds. Both sides should have
   brown spots. Place the cooked tortilla in the
   prepared container.

8. **REPEAT:** Repeat steps 6 and 7 with the
   remaining pieces of dough.

9. **SERVE:** Add your favorite taco fixings
   and enjoy!

FLAKY BUTTERMILK BISCUITS

Yield: 10 large biscuits

PREP TIME: 30 TO 40 MINUTES | **INACTIVE TIME:** 5 TO 10 MINUTES | **BAKE TIME:** 13 TO 15 MINUTES

TOOLS NEEDED: baking sheet, parchment paper, food scale, mixing bowl, spoon, pastry cutter or two forks, rolling pin, 3-inch biscuit cutter (or smaller, for smaller biscuits), pastry brush, toothpick

When it comes to biscuits, the flakier the better, in my opinion. The key to a flaky biscuit or scone is Julia Child's favorite ingredient: butter. These biscuits require plenty of cold butter, and the end result is a delicious, savory biscuit.

520 grams all-purpose flour (3⅓ cups)

80 grams whole-wheat flour (⅔ cup)

20 grams baking powder (1 tablespoon plus 1 teaspoon)

4 grams baking soda (1 teaspoon)

10 grams salt (1½ teaspoons)

226 grams unsalted butter, cold (1 cup)

320 grams buttermilk, chilled, plus extra to brush on tops (1⅓ cups plus 1 tablespoon) (see step 3 of Irish-Inspired Soda Bread on page 16 for how to substitute whole milk)

1. **PREHEAT:** Preheat the oven to 450°F.
2. **PREPARE THE BAKING SHEET:** Line a flat baking sheet with parchment paper.
3. **WEIGH THE INGREDIENTS:** Tare a large mixing bowl; combine the all-purpose flour, whole-wheat flour, baking powder, baking soda, and salt.
4. **STIR:** Stir the dry ingredients together.
5. **ADD THE BUTTER:** Cut the cold butter in half, then cut each half into eight pieces and add to the dry mixture. With two forks or a pastry cutter, cut the butter into the dry ingredients and distribute throughout the dough until crumbly and sandy.
6. **MIX:** Add the chilled buttermilk. Stir until combined and no spots of dry flour remain, being careful not to overmix.
7. **SHAPE:** Turn the dough out onto a floured work surface. Flour a rolling pin and roll the dough out until it is 1 inch thick. Dip a 3-inch biscuit cutter into flour and use it to cut out circles of dough. Place the biscuits on the prepared baking sheet 2 inches apart. Gather the remaining dough scraps and roll out again as many times as necessary to use the rest of the dough. If the butter in the dough is beginning to soften, chill the dough for 20 to 30 minutes in the refrigerator.
8. **BAKE:** Brush additional buttermilk on the tops of the biscuits before they go into the oven. Bake for 13 to 15 minutes, until golden brown and a toothpick inserted in the center of the biscuits comes out clean.
9. **COOL:** Cool for 5 to 10 minutes before serving.

SAVORY SCONES

Yield: 9 scones

PREP TIME: 30 TO 40 MINUTES | **INACTIVE TIME:** 5 TO 10 MINUTES | **BAKE TIME:** 18 TO 20 MINUTES

TOOLS NEEDED: baking sheet, parchment paper, food scale, mixing bowl, spoon, pastry cutter or two forks, rolling pin, toothpick

---

No matter the occasion, these scones will be loved by all your guests. I love these all on their own, but with a fried or poached egg, they also make an incredible breakfast sandwich. With their savory flavors and extra flaky texture, they disappear quickly!

FOR THE DOUGH

400 grams all-purpose flour (2½ cups)

15 grams baking powder (1 tablespoon)

4 grams salt (½ teaspoon)

226 grams unsalted butter, cold (1 cup)

210 grams whole milk, chilled (¾ cup plus 2½ tablespoons)

100 grams sharp cheddar cheese, grated (1 cup, loosely filled)

40 grams cooked bacon, chopped into ¼-inch pieces (about 5 slices)

3 grams fresh chives, minced (1 tablespoon)

1. **PREHEAT:** Preheat the oven to 400°F.
2. **PREPARE THE BAKING SHEET:** Line a flat baking sheet with parchment paper.
3. **WEIGH THE INGREDIENTS:** Tare a mixing bowl; combine the flour, baking powder, and salt.
4. **STIR:** Stir the dry ingredients together.
5. **ADD THE BUTTER:** Cut the cold butter in half, then cut each half into eight pieces and add to the dry mixture. With two forks or a pastry cutter, cut the butter into the dry ingredients and distribute throughout the dough until crumbly and sandy, with no pieces bigger than a pea.
6. **MIX:** Stir in the milk until there are no sections of dry flour remaining; don't overmix. Gently fold in the cheese, bacon, and chives. Fold just until the dough holds together.
7. **SHAPE:** Place the dough on the baking sheet. Roll the dough with a floured rolling pin and pat into an 8½-by-9-inch rectangle that is about 1 inch thick.
8. **DIVIDE:** Cut the rolled dough into 9 pieces that are 3-by-2¾-inch rectangles. Separate the pieces 2 inches apart. Work quickly so that the butter doesn't melt.
9. **BAKE:** Bake for 18 to 20 minutes, until golden brown and a toothpick inserted in the center of the scones comes out clean.
10. **COOL AND SERVE:** Cool for 5 to 10 minutes, then serve.

TIP: Substitute parsley, rosemary, dill, or thyme for the chives.

GRANDMA'S BLUEBERRY CRUMBLE MUFFINS

Yield: 12 muffins

PREP TIME: 20 TO 30 MINUTES | **INACTIVE TIME:** 10 TO 15 MINUTES | **BAKE TIME:** 15 TO 20 MINUTES

TOOLS NEEDED: food scale, 2 large mixing bowls, fork, 2 spoons, small bowl, muffin tin, muffin liners, toothpick

---

Grandma's Blueberry Crumble Muffins is the best version of blueberry muffins I know. They are a reminder of special mornings with my grandparents. I hope they find their way onto your kitchen table as you spend time with the people you love.

FOR THE STREUSEL

28 grams unsalted butter, cold (2 tablespoons)

35 grams brown sugar (2 tablespoons)

35 grams all-purpose flour (3½ tablespoons)

FOR THE BATTER

275 grams all-purpose flour (1¾ cups plus 4 teaspoons)

2 grams baking soda (½ teaspoon)

1 gram salt (¼ teaspoon)

56 grams unsalted butter, at room temperature (¼ cup)

200 grams brown sugar (1 cup)

260 grams full-fat sour cream (1 cup)

1 large egg

4 grams vanilla extract (1 teaspoon)

150 grams blueberries, fresh or frozen (1¼ cups)

1. **PREHEAT:** Preheat the oven to 375°F.
2. **PREPARE THE STREUSEL:** Use a fork to cut and mix the cold butter into the brown sugar and flour. Set aside.
3. **COMBINE THE DRY INGREDIENTS:** In a separate bowl, mix the all-purpose flour, baking soda, and salt. Set aside.
4. **CREAM THE BUTTER AND SUGAR:** Put the butter in a mixing bowl or stand mixer and beat until smooth and creamy. Add the brown sugar and beat until smooth. Stir in the sour cream, egg, and vanilla.
5. **MIX:** Slowly stir the dry ingredients into the wet until combined.
6. **ADD THE BLUEBERRIES:** Fold in the blueberries until they are dispersed throughout the batter.
7. **PREPARE THE MUFFIN TIN:** Place muffin liners in a muffin tin or grease with oil or butter.
8. **FILL THE MUFFIN TIN:** Scoop the batter into the muffin liners, filling until they are three-quarters full. Sprinkle the prepared streusel on top.
9. **BAKE:** Bake for 15 to 20 minutes, until a toothpick or knife inserted into the center of each muffin comes out clean.
10. **COOL:** Cool 10 to 15 minutes before serving.

CALZONES

Yield: 6 medium calzones

PREP TIME: 35 TO 50 MINUTES | **INACTIVE TIME:** 2 TO 2½ HOURS
BAKE TIME: 15 TO 20 MINUTES PER BATCH

TOOLS NEEDED: food scale, large bowl, spoon, plastic dough scraper, baking stone or baking sheet, grater, parchment paper, rolling pin, kitchen scissors, teaspoon, pizza peel or flat cookie sheet, cooling rack, pizza cutter or large knife

Calzones are essentially pizzas folded in half, so they check the box for being delicious while also being a very convenient meal for a party or care package. These calzones are made in the Neapolitan style, with sauce spread on the outside of the crust before baking.

FOR THE DOUGH

310 grams warm water, divided (1¼ cups plus 2 teaspoons)

2 grams instant yeast (½ teaspoon)

6 grams white cane sugar (1 teaspoon)

450 grams bread flour (3 cups plus 3½ tablespoons)

50 grams whole-wheat flour (⅓ cup)

10 grams sea salt (1½ teaspoons)

FOR THE FILLING

16 ounces low-moisture mozzarella cheese

1 (12-ounce) container whole-milk ricotta cheese

4 ounces pepperoni, cut into ¼-inch strips

2 to 3 teaspoons oregano, dried

FOR THE TOPPING

½ cup pizza sauce

½ cup cornmeal

6 tablespoons olive oil

1. **WEIGH THE INGREDIENTS:** Tare a large mixing bowl, then pour in 300 grams of water. Add the yeast and sugar and allow the sugar to dissolve. Add the bread flour and whole-wheat flour.

2. **MIX:** Mix the ingredients together until a shaggy dough forms.

3. **ADD THE SALT:** Tare the bowl of dough, then add the salt. Pour the remaining 10 grams of water over the salt to dissolve it. Continue mixing the dough until all the ingredients are combined.

4. **KNEAD:** Turn the dough out onto a work surface and knead by hand for 8 to 12 minutes or with a dough hook in a stand mixer for 4 to 8 minutes, until the dough no longer sticks to the sides of the bowl and pulls away easily.

5. **BULK FERMENT:** Cover the dough and leave in a warm place for 1½ to 2 hours, until doubled in volume.

6. **PREHEAT:** About 30 minutes before proofing is finished, place a baking stone in the

CONTINUED ON NEXT PAGE

oven. (Use a baking sheet if a baking stone isn't available and make sure to monitor it while baking.) Preheat the oven to 500°F.

7. **DIVIDE THE DOUGH:** Place the dough on a lightly floured work surface and flip it over to get a light coating of flour on both sides. Divide the dough into 6 pieces (about 136 grams each). Pick up each piece and shape by hand into a circular disc. Cover with a cloth to rest while you prepare the filling ingredients.

8. **PREPARE THE FILLING:** Shred the mozzarella cheese. If the ricotta is watery, strain to remove any excess moisture before use. Place the mozzarella, ricotta, pepperoni, oregano, and pizza sauce next to your workstation.

9. **PREPARE THE PEEL TRANSFER:** Place a large square of parchment paper next to where you will be rolling out the dough. Sprinkle with 2 to 3 tablespoons of cornmeal.

10. **ROLL THE DOUGH AND FILL:** Lightly flour the work surface. Roll the dough into a thin circle, about 10 inches wide. Spread 1 to 2 tablespoons of ricotta cheese on one half of the dough, leaving a 1-inch margin. Top with ⅓ cup shredded mozzarella, pepperoni strips, and an additional 2 to 3 tablespoons of mozzarella. Sprinkle ¼ to ½ teaspoon of

oregano over the filling. Take the uncovered half of the dough and stretch it to drape over the filling and meet the other edge of dough. Seal by pressing the seam together with your fingers. Make a small fold into the sealed edge of the dough to reinforce the closure. Use a dough scraper to pick up the calzone and transfer it to the cornmeal-dusted parchment paper. Repeat this step with each piece of dough.

11. **TOP THE CALZONES:** Use kitchen scissors to cut three ½-inch, V-shaped vents on the top of each calzone. Spread 1 teaspoon of pizza sauce over the entire top of each calzone.

12. **BAKE:** Use the pizza peel to transfer 2 to 4 calzones to the hot baking stone. Bake for 15 to 20 minutes, until the crust is crisp and browned. Repeat with the remaining calzones.

13. **COOL AND SERVE:** Slice the calzones without waiting too long so that any steam caught inside doesn't make the crust soggy. After slicing, let them cool for an additional 5 minutes.

14. **SERVE:** Serve the sliced calzones drizzled with 1 tablespoon of olive oil and with extra pizza sauce on the side.

MINI MONKEY BREADS

Yield: 12 mini monkey breads

PREP TIME: 60 TO 75 MINUTES | **INACTIVE TIME:** 2 TO 3 HOURS | **BAKE TIME:** 20 TO 23 MINUTES

TOOLS NEEDED: saucepan or small pot, food scale, large mixing bowl, 3 spoons, plastic dough scraper, 2 small bowls, muffin tin, rolling pin, pizza cutter or knife, butter knife

---

These easy-to-make mini monkey breads are a favorite for celebrating birthdays, sharing at brunch, or enjoying on a weekend morning. The individual portions make them perfectly shareable.

FOR THE DOUGH
180 grams milk (⅔ cup)

30 grams white cane sugar (2 tablespoons)

4 grams instant yeast (1 teaspoon)

350 grams all-purpose flour (2⅓ cups)

3 grams salt (½ teaspoon)

1 large egg

4 grams vanilla extract (1 teaspoon)

1 gram baking powder (¼ teaspoon)

56 grams unsalted butter, melted (¼ cup)

FOR THE TOPPING
¾ cup unsalted butter, melted

1 cup white cane sugar

4 teaspoons ground cinnamon

1. **WARM THE MILK:** Heat the milk until it reaches a temperature of 115°F to 120°F.
2. **WEIGH THE INGREDIENTS:** Tare a large mixing bowl, then pour in 160 grams of warm milk. Add the sugar and instant yeast. Let the sugar dissolve, then add the flour.
3. **MIX:** Mix the ingredients together until a shaggy dough forms, then add the salt, egg, vanilla, and baking powder. Give the mixture 2 to 3 stirs before adding the warm melted butter. Mix to combine.
4. **KNEAD:** Turn the dough out onto a work surface and knead for 10 to 15 minutes by hand or 3 to 7 minutes with a dough hook in a stand mixer on the lowest two speeds, until the dough is smooth, is no longer sticky, and releases easily from the bowl or work surface.
5. **BULK FERMENT:** Cover the dough and allow to ferment for 1½ to 2 hours, until doubled in volume.
6. **PREPARE THE TOPPING:** Place the melted butter in one bowl and combine the sugar and cinnamon in a second small bowl. Place a spoon in each bowl.
7. **PREPARE THE MUFFIN TIN:** Add a generous teaspoon of melted butter to each muffin cup, coating the sides and rims.
8. **SHAPE:** Turn the dough out onto a work surface and roll with a rolling pin into a

CONTINUED ON NEXT PAGE

square (dimensions aren't important) that is ½ inch thick. Use a wheeled pizza cutter or knife to cut the dough into 1-inch-wide vertical strips, then 1-inch-wide horizontal strips, making lots of 1-inch square pieces.

9. **PREPARE THE DOUGH:** Take 5 or 6 pieces of dough at a time and toss with a spoon in the butter. Use the buttered spoon to transfer the dough to the cinnamon-sugar mixture and toss to coat. Transfer the coated pieces to the muffin cups. Repeat this step with all the pieces of dough until the pieces are evenly distributed and brimming over the top of the muffin tin. Pour the rest of the unused melted butter over the dough. Sprinkle the tops with a final teaspoon of cinnamon sugar.

10. **PROOF:** Proof for 30 to 45 minutes, until puffy and an indentation is left when the dough is gently pressed with a fingertip.

11. **PREHEAT:** Preheat the oven to 375°F.

12. **BAKE:** Bake for 15 minutes at 375°F, then lower the temperature to 350°F and bake for an additional 5 to 8 minutes, until the internal temperature of the mini breads is 185°F to 190°F.

13. **COOL:** Cool for 10 to 15 minutes to allow the caramelized sugar to harden, then use a butter knife to remove the breads from the tin.

TWICE-BAKED SEEDED RAISIN BREADS

Yield: 30 to 36 crisp bread slices

PREP TIME: 35 TO 45 MINUTES | **INACTIVE TIME:** 3 TO 5 HOURS
BAKE TIME: 40 TO 50 MINUTES, PLUS 25 TO 33 MINUTES

TOOLS NEEDED: food scale, 2 large mixing bowls, spoon, loaf pan, parchment paper, spatula, toothpick, 2 baking sheets, bread knife

---

Wine and a cheese board are a regular part of special occasions in our family. I love the way this slightly sweet, crisp bread pairs with a strong cheese like blue cheese. These also make an excellent housewarming gift.

---

240 grams all-purpose flour (1⅔ cups)

40 grams whole-wheat flour (⅓ cup)

15 grams baking powder (1 tablespoon)

3 grams salt (½ teaspoon)

280 grams buttermilk (1¼ cups) (see step 3 of Irish-Inspired Soda Bread on page 16 for how to substitute whole milk)

30 grams brown sugar (2 tablespoons)

30 grams maple syrup (2 tablespoons)

115 grams raisins (1 cup)

20 grams flaxseed (1½ tablespoons)

70 grams pumpkin seeds (⅔ cup)

20 grams pecans, roughly chopped (¼ cup)

2 grams fresh rosemary, minced (about 1 teaspoon)

1. **PREHEAT:** Preheat the oven to 400°F.

2. **COMBINE THE DRY INGREDIENTS:** In a mixing bowl, stir together the all-purpose flour, whole-wheat flour, baking powder, and salt. Set aside.

3. **COMBINE THE WET INGREDIENTS:** Pour the buttermilk into a separate mixing bowl. Stir in the brown sugar and maple syrup.

4. **MIX:** Add the dry mixture to the wet mixture. Stir to combine. Add the raisins, flaxseed, pumpkin seeds, pecans, and rosemary. Stir the batter until all the ingredients are well combined.

5. **PREPARE THE LOAF PAN:** Line a loaf pan with a piece of parchment paper. (See step 6 of Zucchini Spice Quick Bread on page 44.)

6. **FILL THE LOAF PAN:** Use a spatula or spoon to transfer the batter to the loaf pan.

7. **BAKE:** Bake for 40 to 50 minutes, until a toothpick or knife inserted into the center of the loaf comes out clean.

8. **COOL:** Allow the loaf to cool completely for 3 to 5 hours. Do not rush this step. Wrap in

CONTINUED ON NEXT PAGE

plastic and chill in the refrigerator once it has cooled to room temperature.

9. **SECOND PREHEAT:** Preheat the oven to 325°F.

10. **PREPARE THE BAKING SHEETS:** Line two baking sheets with parchment paper and set aside.

11. **SLICE:** Use a sharp serrated bread knife to cut ⅛- to ¼-inch-thick slices of bread. Use a heavy weight, like a bag of flour or pots, as a makeshift vice to hold the loaf firmly in place while you are slicing. Lay the slices on the prepared baking sheets.

12. **SECOND BAKE:** Toast the slices in the oven for 15 minutes, then flip and toast for an additional 10 to 18 minutes, until they are golden brown.

13. **COOL:** Allow the slices to cool on the baking sheets.

14. **SERVE:** Serve with cheese or package them as a gift for a friend.

CHEESY ROSEMARY-GARLIC BREAD TWISTS

Yield : 16 twists

PREP TIME: 35 TO 50 MINUTES | **INACTIVE TIME:** 11 TO 15 HOURS | **BAKE TIME:** 20 TO 25 MINUTES

TOOLS NEEDED: food scale, food container, large bowl, spoon, plastic dough scraper, baking sheet, parchment paper, rolling pin, rolling pizza cutter

---

A savory breadstick is a party buffet mainstay but can also serve as a special side for a family dinner. These taste delicious on their own or served with warm marinara sauce.

FOR THE STARTER
15 grams sourdough starter (1 tablespoon) or ⅛ teaspoon instant yeast

110 grams water (7½ tablespoons)

110 grams all-purpose flour (¾ cup)

FOR THE DOUGH
180 grams warm water, divided (¾ cup)

200 grams starter (about 1 cup)

15 grams white cane sugar (1 tablespoon)

3 grams instant yeast (1 teaspoon)

14 grams unsalted butter, at room temperature (1 tablespoon)

370 grams all-purpose flour (2½ cups)

7 grams salt (1 teaspoon)

FOR THE FILLING
70 grams unsalted butter, at room temperature (5 tablespoons)

2 garlic cloves, minced

1 to 2 teaspoons fresh rosemary, minced

70 grams Parmesan cheese, grated (heaping 1 cup, loosely filled)

1. **MAKE THE STARTER:** About 8 to 12 hours before mixing your dough, combine the starter or yeast, water, and flour in a clean container and mix well. Cover and leave at room temperature until bubbly and doubled in volume.

2. **WEIGH THE INGREDIENTS:** Tare a mixing bowl, then pour in 170 grams of warm water. Add 200 grams of starter, the sugar, and the instant yeast. Once the sugar is dissolved, add the butter and the flour.

3. **MIX:** Mix the ingredients together until a shaggy dough forms, then add the salt and the remaining 10 grams of water. Mix to combine.

4. **KNEAD:** Turn the dough out onto a work surface and knead for 10 to 15 minutes by hand or 3 to 7 minutes with a dough hook in a stand mixer on the lowest two speeds, until the dough is smooth, is no longer sticky, and releases easily from the bowl or work surface.

CONTINUED ON NEXT PAGE

5. **BULK FERMENT:** Cover and ferment for 1½ to 2 hours, until doubled in volume.

6. **PREPARE THE BAKING SHEET:** Line a baking sheet with parchment paper and set aside.

7. **PREPARE THE FILLING:** Mix together the butter, garlic, and rosemary.

8. **SHAPE:** On a lightly floured surface, roll the dough into a roughly 16-inch square. Spread the butter mixture on one half of the dough, leaving a ½-inch margin at the very end. Sprinkle the Parmesan over the butter. Fold the unbuttered half of the dough over the cheese and seal the edges together. Use a pizza cutter to cut the dough from the folded edge to the sealed edge into 1-inch-wide strips. Take the ends of a strip, pull slightly to lengthen, and twist 4 or 5 times. Place on the prepared baking sheet and repeat with the remaining strips.

9. **PROOF:** Cover and proof in a warm place for 30 to 60 minutes, until the layers are puffy.

10. **PREHEAT:** Preheat the oven to 400°F.

11. **BAKE:** Bake for 20 to 25 minutes, until the cheese is melted and the bread is golden brown.

12. **COOL:** Let the breadsticks cool for 10 to 20 minutes before serving.

TIP: Instant yeast can be omitted to create a naturally fermented bread. The fermentation and proofing stages will take 2 to 3 times longer if using this method.

WEEKEND CHALLAH BREAD

Yield: 2 medium-size loaves

PREP TIME: 30 TO 45 MINUTES | **INACTIVE TIME:** 12 TO 17 HOURS | **BAKE TIME:** 35 TO 40 MINUTES

TOOLS NEEDED: food scale, food container, large bowl, spoon, plastic dough scraper, 2 baking sheets, parchment paper, steam pan, small bowl, pastry brush, cooling rack

---

Challah has become a well-known bread for many people. It is a Shabbat tradition every Friday for Jewish people. Challah is a favorite bread in our household that symbolizes peace and rest. Hopefully it creates a special atmosphere in your house, as well.

FOR THE STARTER

30 grams sourdough starter (2 tablespoons) or ⅛ teaspoon instant yeast

15 grams white cane sugar (1 tablespoon)

50 grams water (3½ tablespoons)

100 grams all-purpose flour (⅔ cup)

FOR THE DOUGH

100 grams water (about ½ cup)

4 grams instant yeast (1 teaspoon)

150 grams starter (about ¾ cup)

500 grams bread flour (3½ cups)

70 grams oil, such as olive oil or avocado oil (⅓ cup)

70 grams white cane sugar or honey (⅓ cup)

3 large eggs

10 grams salt (1½ teaspoons)

FOR THE EGG WASH

1 large egg

⅛ teaspoon water

Pinch salt

Poppy seeds or sesame seeds, for topping (optional)

1. **MAKE THE STARTER:** About 8 to 12 hours before mixing your dough, combine the starter or yeast, sugar, water, and all-purpose flour in a clean container. Mix to combine, then cover and leave at room temperature until increased in volume and aerated.

2. **WEIGH THE INGREDIENTS:** Making sure to tare after each addition, combine the water, instant yeast, and 150 grams of starter in a large mixing bowl. Add the bread flour.

3. **MIX:** Mix the ingredients together until they form a shaggy dough. Add the oil, sugar, eggs, and salt. Continue mixing until fully combined.

4. **KNEAD:** Turn the dough out onto a work surface and knead for 10 to 15 minutes by hand or 3 to 8 minutes with a dough hook in a stand mixer on the lowest two speeds, until the dough is smooth, is no longer sticky, and releases easily from the bowl or work surface.

CONTINUED ON NEXT PAGE

5. **BULK FERMENT:** Cover the dough and ferment for 2 to 3 hours, until doubled in volume.

6. **PREPARE THE BAKING SHEETS:** Line two baking sheets with parchment paper and set aside.

7. **DIVIDE:** Divide the dough into four equal pieces for two medium loaves.

8. **SHAPE:** Lightly flour a work surface. Take a piece of dough and roll it under your hands into an 18-inch-long rope. Repeat with the remaining pieces of dough. To braid the sections of dough, take two ropes and cross them over each other into an "X" shape. Take the upper two sections of the ropes and pull down toward the bottom so that all four ends are pointed downward. From left to right, think of the pieces of dough as 1, 2, 3, and 4. Bring 1 over 2, 3 over 4, 4 over 1, 2 over 4, 1 over 3, 3 over 2, 4 over 3, and 1 under 2, then tuck all the strands under, pressing the sections to seal them against the bottom of the loaf. The goal of the braiding is to have an alternating and even pattern that comes up higher in the center of the loaf. Hold the ends of the loaf and stretch to even out the shape of the challah.

9. **PROOF:** Place the loaves on the prepared baking sheets to proof. Cover and proof for 45 to 90 minutes, until the loaves have about doubled in size.

10. **PREHEAT:** Near the end of the proofing period, preheat the oven to 375°F and place a steam pan filled with water on the lowest rack.

11. **MAKE THE EGG WASH:** Beat the egg, water, and salt together and brush the egg wash over the tops of the loaves. Sprinkle the loaves with poppy seeds or sesame seeds (if using).

12. **BAKE:** Bake for 25 minutes, then remove the steam pan and continue baking for an additional 10 to 15 minutes, until the loaves are a shiny golden brown.

13. **COOL:** Transfer the challah bread to a cooling rack and cool for 1 hour before serving.

TIP: Instant yeast can be omitted to create a naturally fermented bread. The fermentation and proofing stages will take 2 to 3 times longer if using this method.

CINNAMON-SUGAR PULL-APART BREAD

Yield: 1 shareable loaf

PREP TIME: 40 TO 50 MINUTES | **INACTIVE TIME:** 2 TO 3 HOURS | **BAKE TIME:** 30 TO 38 MINUTES

TOOLS NEEDED: food scale, small pot, large bowl, spoon, plastic dough scraper, loaf pan, parchment paper, 2 small bowls, rolling pin, pastry brush, rolling pizza cutter

---

The center is the absolute best part of a cinnamon roll, and I discovered that this entire cinnamon-sugar pull-apart bread tastes like the center of a cinnamon roll! This is a bread for a weekend brunch, celebrating a birthday, or anytime you want to savor something delicious.

FOR THE DOUGH

110 grams milk (7 tablespoons)

50 grams warm water (3 tablespoons plus 1 teaspoon)

30 grams white cane sugar (2 tablespoons)

4 grams instant yeast (1 teaspoon)

350 grams all-purpose flour (2⅓ cups)

4 grams vanilla extract (1 teaspoon)

1 large egg

3 grams salt (½ teaspoon)

45 grams unsalted butter, melted (3½ tablespoons)

FOR THE FILLING

100 grams white cane sugar (½ cup)

50 grams brown sugar (¼ cup)

3 grams ground cinnamon (1 teaspoon)

30 grams unsalted butter, melted (2¼ tablespoons)

1. **WARM MILK:** Heat the milk until it reaches a temperature of 110°F to 120°F.
2. **WEIGH THE INGREDIENTS:** Tare a large mixing bowl, then pour in 100 grams of warm milk. Add the warm water, sugar, and instant yeast. Once the sugar is dissolved, add the flour.
3. **MIX:** Mix the ingredients together until a shaggy dough forms, then add the vanilla, egg, salt, and slightly warm melted butter. Mix to combine.
4. **KNEAD:** Turn the dough out onto a work surface and knead for 10 to 15 minutes by hand or 3 to 7 minutes with a dough hook in a stand mixer on the lowest two speeds, until the dough is smooth, is no longer sticky, and releases easily from the bowl or work surface.
5. **BULK FERMENT:** Cover and let ferment for 1½ to 2 hours, until doubled in volume.
6. **PREPARE THE LOAF PAN:** Line a loaf pan with parchment paper or grease well.

CONTINUED ON NEXT PAGE

7. **MAKE THE CINNAMON-SUGAR MIXTURE:** Stir together the white sugar, brown sugar, and cinnamon. Set aside.

8. **SHAPE:** On a lightly floured surface, roll out the dough into a 14-by-16-inch rectangle. Brush the melted butter over the dough and sprinkle all the cinnamon-sugar mixture evenly over the top, using your hands to spread it evenly, if needed. Use a pizza cutter or sharp knife to cut the dough in half along the 16-inch length. Place one half on top of the other half. Cut the rectangle stacks in half again along the 7-inch width. Place the divided stacks of two layers on top of each other. Cut in half again to make two stacks of four layers. Place the layers on top of each other again, cut through the middle to create two stacks of eight layers. Cut each stack in half to create four stacks of eight layers. Place the four stacks on their edge in the prepared loaf pan so that they are all in a line. Sprinkle any cinnamon sugar that fell out over the top of the loaf.

9. **PROOF:** Cover and proof in a warm place for 45 to 60 minutes, until the layers are puffy and pressing the dough gently with your finger leaves an indentation.

10. **PREHEAT:** Preheat the oven to 350°F.

11. **BAKE:** Bake for 30 to 38 minutes, until golden brown. Check after 30 minutes; if the top is browning too quickly, tent aluminum foil over the pan.

12. **COOL:** Let the loaf cool for 15 to 20 minutes before removing from the loaf pan and serving.

JALAPEÑO-CHEDDAR SOURDOUGH BREAD

Yield: 1 loaf

PREP TIME: 30 TO 50 MINUTES | **INACTIVE TIME:** 11½ TO 22 HOURS | **BAKE TIME:** 40 MINUTES

TOOLS NEEDED: food scale, food container, large bowl, grater, spoon, plastic dough scraper, parchment paper, bread proofing bowl or colander lined with a kitchen towel, large Dutch oven or steam pan, parchment paper, bread lame or serrated bread knife, spray bottle, cooling rack

This sourdough is full of surprises. With savory cheese and the slow heat of roasted jalapeños, it's fun to make for barbecues, game day, chili cook-offs, or an incredible sandwich. Make sure to use the jarred or canned variety of sliced jalapeños because they have a softer texture and a smokier flavor.

FOR THE STARTER
15 grams sourdough starter (1 tablespoon)

60 grams water (¼ cup)

60 grams all-purpose flour (7 tablespoons)

FOR THE DOUGH
360 grams water, divided (1½ cups plus 2 teaspoons)

100 grams starter (about ½ cup)

100 grams whole-wheat flour (⅔ cup)

400 grams bread flour (2⅔ cups)

10 grams sea salt (1½ teaspoons)

70 grams sharp cheddar cheese, shredded, divided (½ cup, loosely filled)

60 grams canned jalapeño slices, drained (¼ cup)

Rice flour or semolina, for dusting the proofing bowl

1. **REFRESH THE STARTER:** About 6 to 10 hours before mixing your dough, stir together the starter, water, and flour. Cover and leave out at room temperature until it has doubled in volume and become bubbly.

2. **WEIGH THE INGREDIENTS:** Tare a large mixing bowl, then pour in 350 grams water. Add 100 grams of starter, the whole-wheat flour, and the bread flour.

3. **MIX:** Use a spoon or stand mixer to mix everything together until no dry spots of flour remain.

4. **AUTOLYSE:** Cover and let the dough rest for 20 minutes.

5. **ADD THE SALT:** Tare the bowl of dough, then add the salt and very slowly pour the remaining 10 grams of water over the salt to dissolve it. Massage into the dough, rotating and folding the dough to fully incorporate the ingredients.

6. **REST:** Cover and let the dough rest for 30 minutes.

7. **STRETCH AND FOLD:** Place 40 grams of cheddar cheese and the drained jalapeño

slices in the center of the dough. Take the dough in hand and, one-quarter at a time, pull the dough upward, then fold back into the middle. Repeat with the other three quarters. Continue folding until the cheese and jalapeños are well incorporated.

8. **BULK FERMENT:** Cover the dough and ferment at room temperature for 3 to 5 hours, until about doubled in volume.

9. **PRE-SHAPE AND BENCH REST:** Transfer the dough from the bowl onto an unfloured surface. Quickly push the flat end of a dough scraper under one-half of the dough, then fold the dough over itself. Push the scraper under one side of the dough and rotate in a circular motion for 3 to 5 turns until it's a round shape. Leave the dough to rest for 20 minutes.

10. **PREPARE THE PROOFING BOWL:** Dust your proofing bowl generously with rice flour, making sure to coat the sides well.

11. **FINAL SHAPE:** Lightly flour the top of your dough. Push the straight edge of the dough scraper under the whole mound of dough. Guiding with your opposite hand, lift the dough from the work surface and flip it onto its floured side. Place the remaining 30 grams of shredded cheddar cheese in the middle of the dough, then pick up the left and right edges of the dough and fold over the cheese to slightly overlap. Pinch together to seal the seam. Taking the end of the dough below the seam, gently lengthen the dough, then roll it onto itself in a spiral until it seals at the opposite end. The floured side of the dough should be facing up once again. Without flipping the dough over, use a scraper and pull the dough across the work surface or rotate it in a circle until it tightens into a tight ball and you begin to see cheese under the top part of the dough. Quickly slide the dough scraper under the dough to gather the whole round, then flip it into the proofing bowl upside down (floured-side down in the bowl). Cover.

12. **PROOF:** Proof for 1 to 2 hours at room temperature. The dough should rise up the sides of the bowl, and a finger pressed into it should leave an indentation.

13. **PREHEAT:** After 30 to 60 minutes of proofing, preheat the oven to 500°F with the Dutch oven inside on a center rack. If not using a Dutch oven, place a metal pan filled halfway with water on the lowest rack.

14. **BAKE:** Center an extra-long sheet of parchment paper over the proofing bowl. Holding the paper over the bowl by grasping the edges of the bowl, flip it to turn the dough out. Use a bread lame to score the top of your dough with a slit across the top about ¼ inch deep. Carefully pick up the edges of the parchment paper to transfer the dough into the preheated Dutch oven (or onto a baking sheet). Cover with the lid and place the bread in the oven. Spray the walls of the oven with water and shut the door. Reduce the temperature to 460°F and bake for 20 minutes. After 20 minutes, carefully remove the bread from the Dutch oven and place it directly on the oven rack (or remove the steam pan if using). Reduce the heat to 450°F and bake for an additional 20 minutes to create a golden-brown crust.

15. **COOL:** Cool for 1 hour on a rack.

KOREAN-INSPIRED BAO

Yield: 8 buns

PREP TIME: 25 TO 35 MINUTES | **INACTIVE TIME:** 2 TO 3 HOURS | **BAKE TIME:** 12 TO 14 MINUTES

TOOLS NEEDED: food scale, large bowl, spoon, plastic dough scraper, 2-tier bamboo steamer, parchment paper for steaming, rolling pin, chopstick, large wok (or large pot with steaming adapter)

The soft, fluffy texture of these bao buns is a great complement to a spicy filling of Korean barbecue or kimchi. These Korean-inspired bao buns are a fun variation on taco shells and are great for a weekend meal, engagement party, or other event.

200 grams warm water, divided (¾ cup plus 2 tablespoons)

5 grams white cane sugar (1 teaspoon)

6 grams instant yeast (1½ teaspoons)

400 grams all-purpose flour (2⅔ cups)

40 grams arrowroot powder (⅓ cup)

20 grams oil, such as avocado oil, olive oil, or vegetable oil (1 tablespoon plus 1 teaspoon)

4 grams baking powder (½ teaspoon)

4 grams salt (½ teaspoon)

1. **WEIGH THE INGREDIENTS:** Tare a large mixing bowl, then combine 190 grams of warm water, the sugar, and the instant yeast. Allow the sugar to dissolve. Add the flour, arrowroot powder, oil, and baking powder.

2. **MIX:** Mix the ingredients together until a shaggy dough forms, then add the salt and the remaining 10 grams of warm water. Mix to combine.

3. **KNEAD:** Turn the dough out onto a work surface and knead for 10 to 15 minutes by hand or 5 to 8 minutes with a dough hook in a stand mixer on the lowest two speeds, until very smooth.

4. **BULK FERMENT:** Cover and let the dough ferment for 1½ to 2 hours, until doubled in volume.

5. **PREPARE THE STEAMER:** Line two bamboo steam trays with a round sheet of

parchment made for bamboo steamers and set aside.

6. **DIVIDE:** Divide the dough into 8 equal pieces (about 41 grams each) and roll each piece into a ball. Cover with a cloth to keep the dough from drying out.

7. **SHAPE:** Roll a ball into a 3-inch circle that is ¼ to ½ inch thick. Lay a chopstick across the middle, then fold the dough over the chopstick, keeping the space open in the middle. Pull out the chopstick. Place the folded bao bun into the prepared steamer (4 in each tray, separating with parchment or muffin liners if necessary). Repeat with the rest of the dough.

8. **PROOF:** Stack the bamboo steam trays and cover. Proof the bao buns for 30 to 45 minutes, until puffy.

9. **HEAT THE WOK:** Place a large wok filled with 2 to 3 inches of water on the stovetop. Bring the water to a boil.

10. **STEAM:** Place the closed bamboo steamer into the wok and steam for 12 to 14 minutes over medium-low heat. After 10 minutes, rotate the steamer tray layers for even steaming. The bottom of the steamer should stay submerged in water, but the water should reach no higher than ¼ inch up the side. After 12 to 14 minutes, turn off the heat and let the buns sit covered for an additional 5 to 10 minutes.

11. **SERVE:** Serve fresh with your favorite fillings.

MINI PAIN D'ÉPI

Yield: 4 mini pain d'épi

PREP TIME: 25 TO 40 MINUTES | **INACTIVE TIME:** 11½ TO 22 HOURS | **BAKE TIME:** 18 TO 20 MINUTES

TOOLS NEEDED: food scale, food container, large bowl, spoon, plastic dough scraper, baking sheet, parchment paper, steam pan, kitchen scissors, spray bottle, cooling rack

---

Mini Pain d'Épi look like a wheat stalk and are in a small, manageable size that is perfect for a beautiful charcuterie board. The cut sections that look like spikes of wheat on a stalk are perfect for tearing off and enjoying with some cheese.

FOR THE STARTER
15 grams sourdough starter (1 tablespoon)
60 grams water (¼ cup)
60 grams all-purpose flour (7 tablespoons)

FOR THE DOUGH
330 grams water, divided (1⅓ cups plus 1 tablespoon)
100 grams whole-wheat flour (⅔ cup)
400 grams bread flour (2⅔ cups)

100 grams starter (about ½ cup)
10 grams sea salt (1½ teaspoons)

1. **REFRESH THE STARTER:** About 6 to 10 hours before mixing your dough, stir together the starter, water, and flour. Cover and leave at room temperature until doubled.
2. **WEIGH THE INGREDIENTS:** Tare a large mixing bowl, then combine 320 grams of water, the whole-wheat flour, and the bread flour.
3. **MIX:** Using a spoon, mix all the ingredients together.
4. **AUTOLYSE:** Cover and let the dough rest for 20 minutes.
5. **ADD THE STARTER:** Tare the weight of the bowl, then add 100 grams of starter. Massage the starter into the dough until distributed throughout.
6. **ADD THE SALT:** Tare the bowl again, then add the salt and very slowly pour the remaining

10 grams of water over the salt to dissolve it. Massage and fold until fully combined.
7. **KNEAD:** Turn the dough out onto a work surface and knead for 5 to 10 minutes by hand or 3 to 6 minutes with a dough hook in a stand mixer on the lowest two speeds. This dough is meant to be stiff, but if it is too dry, add additional water 1 teaspoon at a time.
8. **BULK FERMENT:** Allow the dough to ferment at room temperature for 3 to 7 hours, until doubled in volume.
9. **DIVIDE:** Transfer the dough to an unfloured surface and divide into 4 pieces using the sharp edge of a dough scraper (about 232 grams each).
10. **PRE-SHAPE AND BENCH REST:** Take a piece of dough and, using the dough scraper, fold

one half of the dough over the top and push it into a log shape. Repeat with the remaining pieces of dough. Let rest for 20 minutes.

11. **PREPARE THE BAKING SHEET:** Line a baking sheet with parchment paper and set aside.

12. **SHAPE:** Lightly flour the work surface and the top of one of the pre-shaped pieces of dough. Use the straight edge of the dough scraper to flip the dough over so that the sticky, unfloured side is facing up. Use your hands to gently stretch the dough into a rectangular shape. Fold the top edge of the dough into the middle of the sticky side. Take the bottom edge and fold it into the sticky center on top of the other edge of dough and pinch along the seam to seal. Finally, gently roll the dough with your hands, pulling outward to elongate the dough to 12½ to 13 inches long with even thickness. Transfer the shaped dough to the prepared baking sheet, seam-side down. Repeat with the remaining pieces of dough, spacing them 3 to 4 inches apart.

13. **PROOF:** Proof uncovered for 30 to 60 minutes at room temperature, until a finger gently pressed into the dough leaves an indentation. Loosely cover and place the baking sheet in the refrigerator for 30 to 60 minutes while the oven preheats.

14. **PREHEAT:** Preheat the oven to 500°F with a steam pan filled with water on the lowest rack.

15. **FINAL SHAPE:** Use kitchen scissors to cut sections of the dough every 1½ inches at a 45-degree angle along the length of the loaves, leaving the bottom of the dough intact. After every cut, move the cut section of dough to the side, flared out, alternating which side you move the dough to each time. The final shape will look like a wheat stalk.

16. **BAKE:** Place the baking sheet in the hot oven. Quickly spray a mist of water over the dough and on the oven walls and close the door. Reduce the temperature to 475°F and bake for 12 minutes. After 12 minutes, remove the steam pan and bake for an additional 6 to 8 minutes, until the crust hardens and turns golden brown.

17. **COOL:** Place on a cooling rack for 30 minutes to cool before serving.

TIP: To substitute commercial yeast for the sourdough starter, mix 60 grams of flour, 60 grams of water, and ⅛ teaspoon of instant yeast. Add 3 grams of additional instant yeast in step 2. Adjust the bulk ferment time to 1½ to 3 hours and proof for 30 to 90 minutes.

Preparing Kanelbullar, page 83

MEASUREMENT CONVERSIONS

	US STANDARD	US STANDARD (OUNCES)	METRIC (APPROXIMATE)
VOLUME EQUIVALENTS (LIQUID)	2 tablespoons	1 fl. oz.	30 mL
	¼ cup	2 fl. oz.	60 mL
	½ cup	4 fl. oz.	120 mL
	1 cup	8 fl. oz.	240 mL
	1½ cups	12 fl. oz.	355 mL
	2 cups or 1 pint	16 fl. oz.	475 mL
	4 cups or 1 quart	32 fl. oz.	1 L
	1 gallon	128 fl. oz.	4 L
VOLUME EQUIVALENTS (DRY)	⅛ teaspoon	————	0.5 mL
	¼ teaspoon	————	1 mL
	½ teaspoon	————	2 mL
	¾ teaspoon	————	4 mL
	1 teaspoon	————	5 mL
	1 tablespoon	————	15 mL
	¼ cup	————	59 mL
	⅓ cup	————	79 mL
	½ cup	————	118 mL
	⅔ cup	————	156 mL
	¾ cup	————	177 mL
	1 cup	————	235 mL
	2 cups or 1 pint	————	475 mL
	3 cups	————	700 mL
	4 cups or 1 quart	————	1 L
	½ gallon	————	2 L
	1 gallon	————	4 L
WEIGHT EQUIVALENTS	½ ounce	————	15 g
	1 ounce	————	30 g
	2 ounces	————	60 g
	4 ounces	————	115 g
	8 ounces	————	225 g
	12 ounces	————	340 g
	16 ounces or 1 pound	————	455 g

	FAHRENHEIT (F)	CELSIUS (C) (APPROXIMATE)
OVEN TEMPERATURES	250°F	120°C
	300°F	150°C
	325°F	165°C
	350°F	180°C
	375°F	190°C
	400°F	200°C
	425°F	220°C
	450°F	230°C

RESOURCES

- **Breadtopia**
  Breadtopia.com
  A source for bread-baking tools, starters, flour, and grain.

- **LivingBreadBaker.com**
  My site, where you can learn how to make your own sourdough starter, find out about online classes, and more.

- **Sourdough.co.uk**
  Studies and information about the digestibility of sourdough.

INDEX

ACKNOWLEDGMENTS

Thank you to the team at Callisto Media for your guidance and support through the writing process. Special thanks to Brian Sweeting for thorough edits, the developmental and copy editors, the design team, the photographers and styling team, and the marketing team.

Brandon, I could not have done this without your encouragement and practical help. I am so thankful we get to do life together and support each other in pursuing big dreams and goals.

Aaron, Daniella, and James, you three are the best encouragers. I'm so thankful we get to start our own traditions. Thank you for being patient with this long writing process. I know it's been a sacrifice for you, and I pray that you see the fruit of these endeavors someday.

Thank you to my family (Mom, Dad, Ashton, and JP) for cheering me on, supporting me, taste testing, and watching kids.

I am forever grateful for "the bread of life," Jesus Christ. Just like the miracle of feeding the 5,000, my continued prayer is that I and anyone I teach can bring the joy and wonder of living bread to our homes and communities.

Much of this book was written through the most difficult period we have faced as a world. I am immensely grateful to the farmers, ranchers, and grocers who feed our families and made it possible to make and test the recipes in this book.

Thank you to my friends who supported me, prayed for me, helped me with recipe taste testing, shared bread flour during the shortages, or offered cultural insights on bread. Thank you, Hannah, Ashley, Mary, Becca, Melyssa, Kirsten, Kylie, Lori, Jenny, Olivia, Selena, Sharon, Rachael, Charity, Laura, Jordanna, Cheri, my CBS Bible study, and my neighbors.

ABOUT THE AUTHOR

 **Jenny Prior** is a mom of three, an avid bread baker, and a passionate teacher. She owns and operates a business in Northern California called Living Bread Baker to teach others about sourdough baking. She delights in seeing people connect with family and friends through her baking classes as they discover joy in a newfound skill.

CPSIA information can be obtained
at www.ICGtesting.com
Printed in the USA
LVHW011058241020
669638LV00004B/4